MARXISM / STRUCTURALISM / EDUCATION:

Theoretical Developments in the Sociology of Education

Madan Sarup

Goldsmiths' College
University of London

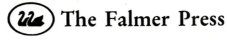 **The Falmer Press**

A member of the Taylor & Francis Group
London and New York

First published 1983

ISBN 0905273 55 9 limp
0905273 56 7 cased

Jacket design by Leonard Williams

Typeset in 11/13 Garamond
by Imago Publishing Ltd, Thame, Oxon

Printed and bound by Taylor & Francis (Printers) Ltd
Basingstoke
for
The Falmer Press
(*A Member of the Taylor & Francis Group*)
Falmer House
Barcombe, Lewes
Sussex BN8 5DL
England

MARXISM / STRUCTURALISM / EDUCATION

By the same author:

Marxism and Education
Education, State and Crisis

Contents

**For Eileen
With Love**

How could you find anything beautiful if you looked at it forever? You'd grow tired of it. Why fall in love if it lasted forever? When you'd forgiven yourselves a thousand times you'd tire of forgiveness. You'd grow tired of changing the people you loved. If you ate for eternity why bother to taste what you're eating? You can taste the next meal. When you've cried for one mistake you wouldn't cry for the next. You'd have eternity to put it right. Soon your eyes would be full of sleep. You'd go deaf. You wouldn't listen to voices because they would give the trouble of answering. Why listen to them? It would be useless to know which was a bird or a waterfall. In eternity there would be no future. You'd sit on the ground and turn to stone. Dust would pile up and bury you. If we didn't die we'd live like the dead. Without death there's no life. No beauty, love or happiness. You can't laugh for more than a few hours or weep more than a few days. No one could bear more than one life. Only hell could be eternal. Sometimes life is cruel and death is sudden — that's the price we pay for not being stones. Don't let the lightning strike you or madmen burn your house. Don't give yourself to your enemies or neglect anyone in need. Fight.

Edward Bond, Summer

Acknowledgements

To assimilate the exciting and rapid developments in the sociology of education students are under pressure to come to terms with some very different, complex and demanding intellectual traditions. To understand Althusser, a return to Marx and the long history of the debates about humanist marxism is necessary; to comprehend structuralism and semiology one must read Saussure; to grasp Lacanian theory one must go back to Freud. My students at Goldsmiths' College asked for an introductory course on these approaches and this book is a product of our joint exploration. I wish to express my thanks to them and to all the authors cited in the *Notes*. I should also like to thank Elsa Adamowicz and Peter Dunwoodie for spending many hours discussing the ideas contained in this book, and to Peter Dews, Terry Eagleton, Anne Kampendonk and Richard Winter for their helpful comments on sections of the draft.

Introduction: Education and Textbooks

The Dominant Educational Paradigm

When considering state education and its institutionalization in the nineteenth century, it must not be thought that the English bourgeoisie was in favour of working-class 'education' *in general*; actually, it was only interested in teaching *specific* things in a specific way. Schooling was aimed at changing the attitudes and shaping the conduct of the working class by the provision of bourgeois theories, morals, and religious codes. The placing of a middle-class teacher *in loco parentis*, for example, was an attempt to ensure that the child got a proper moral training in the place of 'bad' parental working-class upbringing.[1] Working-class people, besides being made into a punctual, disciplined labour force, had to be 'uplifted' in order to stabilize the political and social order.[2]

Things have not changed much since then. I believe that the educational system is completely divorced from the needs and interests of children.[3] It is hardly surprising that under these circumstances school is experienced as an imposition by many working-class youngsters. The compulsory nature of the school and the content of the curriculum are serious problems for many young people. Kids, faced with the coercive form and content of schools, 'mess about' in class and cause trouble. Often this is not recognized by teachers as a form of resistance.

Why is education unpopular? Perhaps a part of the answer lies in the nature of the dominant paradigm in education. What are its main characteristics? There is no doubt that the social democratic paradigm, through workings of the 'selective tradition' — the process by which certain meanings and practices are chosen for emphasis and others are neglected, excluded, diluted, or reinterpreted — places a stress on 'amelioration', the equalization of 'access'. Ostensibly, there is a policy of increasing 'equal opportunity' in education, but student or worker control of any institution is never considered.

Another characteristic of the social democratic paradigm is its unwillingness to discuss the topic of class conflict in an open manner in the school curriculum. The 'hidden curriculum' actually serves to reinforce 'the basic rules' surrounding the nature of conflict and its uses. It posits a network of assumptions that establishes, when internalized by students, the boundaries of legitimacy.[4] The basic assumption is that conflict is to be 'resolved' within accepted boundaries and that changes in the framework and rules of institutional arrangements are not desirable. Since change and conflict are systematically neglected, students are presented with a view that serves to legitimate the existing social order.

Furthermore, the social democratic educational system presents itself as neutral and attempts to turn conflicts and disagreements into 'administrative' problems. How is this done? The educational apparatus increasingly makes use of systems-management procedures in its institutions. More and more spheres of educational decision-making are perceived as technical problems that only necessitate instrumental strategies by 'neutral' experts, hence effectively removing the decisions from the field of political debate.[5] In other words, political and ethical issues are converted into engineering puzzles. In this way social problems are depoliticized. Of course, the experts in the educational uses of systems logic assume that their procedures are merely 'scientific' (interest-free) techniques. But this is not so, their procedures are used to maintain social control.

Through the workings of this 'liberal' educational system, in the ways outlined above, children learn to accept as natural the social distinctions schools teach between important and unimportant knowledge, between normality and deviance, between work and play. This is, of course, how ideology operates — through the control of meaning, through the manipulation of the very categories and modes of thinking we commonsensically use. The meanings and practices act to saturate our consciousness so that the economic, political, and educational world we see and interact with becomes the only possible world. It should not be forgotten, though, that there is always some resistance to this process.

One important way in which meanings are controlled is through textbooks. I have examined many of the books recommended in sociology courses, and I have found that most textbooks adopt one of the following ways of looking at education: the 'problems' approach, the 'conflict' approach, and the 'structural contradictions' approach. Let us briefly consider these perspectives.

The 'Problems' Approach

The problems approach focusses on discrete problems and then widens out to an attempt to find a suitable explanatory theory. Many textbooks in this category consist of a loose, disparate collection of topics which have little coherence. Underlying the problems is the implicit assumption that education is a homeostatic system and that it has a natural and moral order. Whilst the main feature of the natural order is competition, the main characteristic of the political order is *consensus.* From this it follows that there is a stress on the prevention of dislocation (or 'dysfunction') in the educational system. It is held that institutions within the system can be isolated and studied in themselves. Though this approach (widely used in the USA) has produced some useful studies of schools, its main inadequacy is that it takes the capitalist market economy for granted and tends to ignore questions concerning conflict and power.

The 'Conflict' Approach

The conflict approach focusses on how schooling expresses patterns of inequality. Social scientists who work within this approach (for example, A.H. Halsey and J.W.B. Douglas) tend to ask questions like: Why are there such inequalities of achievement in education? Why do working-class children persistently underachieve? Though this approach is useful in that it asks 'who gets what?', it has some shortcomings. It falls into the trap of believing that resources are 'scarce' and, like the first approach, reflects rather than challenges the *status quo.*

In my view the values expressed in most textbooks are, on the whole, those which the ruling classes consider essential to transmit.[6] While I was looking at some books selected as school texts recently, I noticed that certain themes do emerge more often than others. Many school texts, for example, imply that we should regard the poor as responsible for their own poverty, the poorly educated as responsible for their lack of education. Such situations are seen as a consequence of the failure of *individuals* rather than the failure of society to

3

distribute educational resources universally. This ideology, usually associated with 'liberalism' or 'social democracy', encourages those actions that attempt to change the individual, while leaving the unequal economic structures intact. It could be said, in short, that this social democratic approach separates the discussion of social justice, the distribution of education, from the mode of production.

The 'Structural Contradictions' Approach

This approach, based on the use of marxist concepts, asks funda-mental questions, such as: Why is it said that resources for education are 'scarce'? Why and how does 'scarcity' arise? It analyzes schooling in terms of the social, political, and *economic* relations of society and insists that many of the problems in schools are a manifestation of the deeper structural contradictions of capitalism.

But what do I mean by 'structural'? Now, it could be said that Marx, like Freud and Saussure, was a precursor in some ways of present-day structuralism. What they have in common and what they share with present-day structuralists is a conviction that surface events and phenomena are to be explained by structures, data and phenomena below the surface. There is, therefore, an attempt to uncover deep structures, unconscious motivations, *underlying causes*. One of the aims of this book is to explain and analyze the structuralist approach.

Now, it seems to me that one of the reasons why education is unpopular is that most of the subjects in the school curriculum are taught in an irrelevant way. In the teaching of history, for example, so-called 'facts' are stressed; the whole emphasis is on the actions of individuals, on 'who did what'. A liberal, humanist view of history is presented in most schools.[7] In the teaching of English, though some pupils are allowed scope for an imaginative exploration of language, the dominant codes continue to be transmitted. Literature, like most subjects in school, is taught as if it existed outside history. There are historical crises, but in the teaching of literature these are not referred to. If a crisis is mentioned, it is always a personal one.

In short, school knowledge is regarded as 'given' and neutral, school subjects are presented as apolitical and ahistorical. The com-plex nexus of political and economic power that lies behind curri-culum organization and selection remains hidden. Moreover, knowledge is increasingly divided into separate, fragmented and competing disciplines. A certain form of narrow thinking is fostered;

concepts such as fact/value, cause/effect, freedom/necessity, nature/culture, reason/emotion are treated as absolute opposites rather than dialectically related.

How, then, should history, literature, social and cultural studies be taught? This is one of the main concerns of the first part of this book. The first three chapters are an exploration of the disjunction between theories that stress experience of human beings (humanism) and those that stress historical and structural determinations. Chapter 1 begins with an outline of the differing conceptions of society that are held by marxists, and there is then an exposition of Althusser's views on ideology and the school as an ideological state apparatus. This prepares the ground for the controversy discussed in the chapters that follow between humanist and structuralist approaches. Chapter 2 is an introduction to the debate about the role of the human subject in history. Chapter 3 is a continuation of the debate in relation to literature. The teaching of these subjects is briefly examined and it is argued that teachers should have a thorough knowledge of these debates, that they should be more aware of the underlying assumptions, the implications and possible consequences of the theoretical approaches they use in their teaching.

Chapter 1

Ideology and Schooling

'Expressive' and 'Structural' Social Totality

Humanist marxism and structuralist marxism are opposing problematics; they have different conceptions of society, history, class, ideology, and literature. It is important to realize that humanism and structuralism are *traditions* and that many theorists have contributed to their development. Georg Lukács, Antonio Gramsci, Jean Paul Sartre, for example, are usually placed in the humanist category; Louis Althusser, Nicos Poulantzas, Pierre Macherey are considered structuralist marxists. Let me sketch in broad outline the two positions. I will take Lukács to embody humanist marxism and Althusser to represent structuralist marxism.

Humanism, to put it simply, can be defined as a theory which seeks to explain society and history by taking as its starting point human essence, the free human subject, the subject of needs, of work, the subject of moral and political action. Humanists such as Lukács see history as a process of becoming, through which the world view of a class attains its full expression.

Lukács' main ideas are expressed in *History and Class Consciousness*.[1] Everything in capitalism, he argues, is made to be sold, all production is for the market. The 'commodity form' permeates everything. Even relationships between people take on the appearance of things. This is the meaning of *reification*. With superb insight Lukács also writes about the fragmentation of the work process and how it is controlled by capital. He describes how rationalization and calculation pervade every aspect of life and how capital uses these processes and techniques to have power over us.

But how is this coercive and exploitative system to be overcome? The answer is the proletariat. For Lukács the crucial link between marxism and the proletariat is class consciousness; but to fully comprehend the role of the proletariat one has to understand Lukács' Hegelian view of history, according to which each social totality or society has a single principle. All phenomena of any one epoch (its philosophy, its art and literature) are merely expressions of this inner principle or essence. For that reason opponents call the Lukácsian humanist view (pejoratively) 'essentialist'.

In Hegel's theory, spirit (*Geist*) is continuously objectivating itself through History in a sequence of distinct stages. Later, Dilthey adapted the Hegelian idea and argued that each period, each society, had its own world outlook (*Weltanschauung*). These ideas were further developed by Lukács, who replaced Hegel's unfolding *Geist* with the proletariat. For Lukács class consciousness is the essence of the proletariat, the 'universal' class. Humanism is thus often associated with historicism: the idea that there is an all-embracing teleological process in which the historical subject realizes its self-positing end. Lukács accepts this teleological view of history, in which a particular class is seen as the creative subject of history.

What, then, are the chief characteristics of humanist marxism? It can be said that it is against any deterministic or functionalist account of the social world. Humanists, reacting against the mechanistic and reductionist theories of an economistic marxism, tend to stress culture and the value of the agents. The stress is on getting inside the mind, the feelings, and the rationalities of the agents themselves. In short, priority is given to the portrayal of *lived experience*. Experience defines both the object and the method of inquiry. The quality of human relationships is emphasized rather than the actual structuring of the relations by external forces. Moreover, humanism tends to be voluntaristic, that is to say, it emphasizes the activist elements, the 'class for itself'. There are, for example, some contemporary humanist marxists (like E.P. Thompson) who, as we shall see in the next chapter, focus not on the structures of exploitation but rather on forms of resistance as if they were an expression of some 'essential' humanity.

What is the Althusserian critique of Lukács and the humanist tradition? First it must be made clear that both Lukács and Althusser argue against any simple 'base and superstructure' view of society, according to which everything in society is determined by the economic 'base'. When the forces and relations in the mode of production change, then the 'superstructure' (for example, politics, law, even philosophy and art) changes also. Such a mechanistic view is sometimes ascribed to Engels and Plekhanov. Lukács *and* Althusser are highly critical of this 'reflectionist' theory because of the economic reductionism that results from it. It is a theory in which the superstructure is reduced to an epiphenomenon of the economic base. In this conceptualization the movement from the base to the super-structure is always unidirectional, unilateral, and social processes tend to be seen as rigid laws. The base/superstructure metaphor is rather simplistic because there is no notion of contradiction, and it is crude because the mediations are missing.

But Althusser is *also* antagonistic to Lukács' Hegelian concep-tion of the 'expressive totality', in which aspects of the superstructure are phenomenal forms of an 'essence'. In order to make the debate clearer, let me elaborate on the humanist and structuralist concep-tions of social totality.

It has often been said that western marxism was from the 1930s through to the 1960s dominated by the influence of Hegel. Althusser opposes all Hegelian interpretations and refers to the Lukácsian conception of the social whole as an 'expressive totality'. He defines this as a totality whose parts are conceived as 'so many "total parts", each expressing the others, and each expressing the social totality that contains them, because each in itself contains in the immediate form of its expression the essence of the social totality itself.'[2] At the centre of the totality is an essential contradiction, which is usually construed as the conflict between the new, dynamic *forces* of economic produc-tion and the restraining hand of the old social *relations* of production. This essential contradiction is then said to be present in, and therefore capable of being 'read off' from, each of the constituent parts which comprise the social totality.

Althusser contends that the social totality should be viewed as consisting of a number of distinct but interrelated 'instances' or 'levels' of practical activity. The social formation is complex, made up of the economic, the political, ideological and theoretical levels. These levels are determining and determined; there is 'relative autonomy' between and within the levels. Althusser insists that the social formation is not just a matter of intersubjective relations between people. We are bearers, supports, of the relations of production; and determination, in the last instance, is by the economic level. In this formulation, change results not from the working out of a basic or simple contradiction, such as that between the forces and relations of production, but from the overlapping of a number of distinct, relatively autonomous contradictions in a particular historical con-juncture. Revolutions occur when there is a fusion, a condensation of a multiplicity of contradictions. Let us now turn to a discussion of

Althusser's contribution to the marxist theory of ideology, focussing particularly on his view of education.

Ideology: The Contribution of Althusser

The term 'ideology' is used to designate a set of ideas, or a body of beliefs, and usually refers to some aspects of the process by which subjects know the world. But the trouble with giving any definition such as the above is that the word 'ideology' is now used in so many different ways that we no longer know what the speaker or writer means by it.[3] One sense of 'ideology' refers to false consciousness, upside-down reality, 'mere illusion'. Another sense of 'ideology' is the set of ideas which arises from a given set of material interests — a system of ideas appropriate to a certain class.[4]

Though Marx used the term extensively — his use of it is always concrete, specific, polemical — there is no formal analysis of it in his work. It is partly because there is no well-founded or finished theory of ideology in Marx and Engels that the area has become a contentious one. Not only are there different interpretations of what Marx meant by the term at different stages of his life, but some writers — Lukács, Gramsci, Althusser, and others — have proposed different and often contradictory ways of comprehending ideology. Giving definitions of ideology is useless, because these marxists have constructed *theories of ideology* which have to be understood in the context of their general contributions to the development of western marxism.[5]

The work of Lukács is usually associated with the view that ideology is a form of false consciousness imposed from above upon the individual by the dominant class. His writings, however, also contain a move from the original negative sense of ideology (as a distortion) to the view that ideology is a set of ideas which express the interests of a class. There is a shift from a discussion of 'ideology' to 'class ideologies'. And so, just as there is 'bourgeois ideology', there is 'marxist ideology' which serves class interests. For Lukács ideology becomes a class view, a *Weltanschauung*. Ideology is identified with class consciousness — the imputed consciousness of a social class which is determined by the place it occupies in the relations of production.

This theory is being increasingly questioned by structuralist marxists like Althusser, who argue that ideology has a material existence which determines the human subject (the individual).

Althusser argues that ideology is a practice producing human subjects. The subject is not the originating source of consciousness, but a product of a specific practice. In Althusser's conception, social agents are not the constitutive subjects of their acts, but supports of the structures.

Let us now consider Althusser's enormously influential paper 'Ideology and Ideological State Apparatuses', in which these views are expressed.[6] He begins his essay by stating that, in order to exist, every social formation must reproduce firstly, the productive forces, and secondly, the existing relations of production. The infrastructure is the economic base (the unity of the productive forces and the relations of production). The superstructure has two levels or 'instances'. At one level there is the law and the state; at the other level there are different ideologies, the religious, legal, ethical, political, and so forth. Obviously, this is a metaphor; the upper floors could not 'stay up' if they did not rest on the base.[7] There is relative autonomy in the superstructure. That is to say, there is reciprocal action (not causation) of the superstructure on the base. There are contradictions within each level, the economic, the political, the ideological, and the theoretical; but determination in the last instance is by the economic base. In other words, there is not a simple dialectic of economic base and superstructure, but a complex unity of separate and specific levels of practice which may be relatively autonomous.

Let me make this clearer. Althusser denies that the economic position of the subject acts as the origin of its ideological position, and so ideology cannot be simply 'read off' from the position of subjects as economic agents. Nevertheless the economy is determinant in that it determines which of the levels of the social formation occupies the dominant place in any mode of production. Althusser regards ideology as an effect of the structure, and the subjects of this structure act as mere supports for it. He insists that ideology has a material existence in the social formation and exists not as a series of ideas, but in a complex set of practices. Ideologies are not merely reflections in the psyche but are lived; they actually structure the real actions of human beings.

Althusser emphasizes that an ideology always exists in an apparatus and its practices; this existence is material. He writes of people acting according to ideas they hold, that is to say, of actions inserted into practices governed by the rituals within the material existence of an ideological apparatus. He then makes the following points: (1) there is no practice except by and in an ideology; (2) there is no ideology except by the subject or for subjects. In other words,

Althusser challenges humanism by rejecting the notion of the constitutive subject and proposes, instead, the constitution of the subject by ideology.[8] In his view ideology is a functional requirement of society which constitutes subjects.

Althusser insists that human beings cannot live without a certain representation of their world and of their relations to it. Ideology is an essential element of all societies as it secures fulfilment of certain social tasks: 'historical materialism cannot conceive that even a communist society could ever do without ideology'.[9] Ideology, then, is a structural feature of any society, its function is the cementing of its unity. In a class society ideology has a further function; it is a means of maintaining domination of one class over the others. Thus Althusser arrives at the concept of dominant and dominated ideologies. The dominated formulate their grievances in the language and logic of the dominant class. That is why the working class cannot liberate itself from bourgeois ideology, but needs to receive from outside the help of science.

Althusser argues that there is a radical epistemological break between ideology and science. Ideological theoretical practice is a pre-scientific mode of cognition, it formulates false problems; scientific theoretical practice, on the other hand, poses the problem in an entirely different manner. Science constitutes itself by breaking with ideology at the moment of its inception. Ideology can be unmasked by science, but ideology will always subsist.

Althusser also distinguishes between a 'theory of ideology in general' and 'theories of particular ideologies'. Particular ideologies exist in concrete societies with specific forms of class struggle; they therefore have a history. 'Ideology in general', however, has no history; it is eternal, exactly like Freud's concept of the unconscious.[10]

The School As an Ideological State Apparatus

Althusser explicitly conceives of the state as a repressive apparatus consisting of the police, the army, prisons and courts, government and administration. Making a distinction between state power and state apparatus, Althusser argues that the objective of the class struggle is state power. The proletariat must seize it and replace it with a proletarian apparatus. Ultimately the aim is to destroy the state, end state power and every apparatus.[11]

There is one Repressive State Apparatus, but there are many

Ideological State Apparatuses (ISAs). The former functions mainly by repression and violence, the latter mainly by ideology. *Many subtle combinations* may be woven from the interplay of the above. No class can hold state power without exercising hegemony over and in the ISAs.[12] All ISAs contribute towards the same result: the reproduction of the relations, the capitalist relations of production. Each of the ideological state apparatuses contributes towards this single result in the way proper to it.

Althusser contends that the ISA which has been installed in a dominant position in mature capitalist social formations is the educational ideological apparatus. Indeed, the School-Family couple has replaced the Church-Family couple. After all, no other ideological state apparatus has the obligatory and free audience of all children in the capitalist social formation, eight hours a day for five days a week. Althusser asks, what do children learn at school? They learn 'know-how'. 'But besides these techniques and knowledges, and in learning them, children at school also learn the "rules" of good behaviour ... rules of respect for the socio-technical division of labour and ultimately the rules of the order established by class domination.'[13] The school, always presented as a neutral environment,

> takes children from every class at infant-school age, and then for years in which the child is most 'vulnerable', squeezed between the family state apparatus and the educational state apparatus, it drums into them, whether it uses new or old methods, a certain amount of 'know-how' wrapped in the ruling ideology in its pure state.[14]

In this system each mass of children ejected en route is practically provided with the ideology which suits the role it has to fulfil in class society. But Althusser reminds us that though the ISAs function predominantly by ideology, there is no such thing as a purely ideological apparatus; they also function secondarily by repression. Thus schools and churches use suitable methods of punishment, expulsion, selection, etc. to discipline not only their shepherds but also their flocks.[15]

Althusser emphasizes that it is more and more the capitalist education system that provides the reproduction of labour power. This labour power must of course be 'appropriate'; the labourers must have a certain level of skills, distributed according to the requirements of the social and technical division of labour.

An Example from Student Training

Before making some criticisms of Althusser, I would like to give an example of a *particular* ideology. This section exemplifies Althusser's view that ideas are real because they are always inscribed in social practices. Ideas are expressed in objective social forms. Individuals 'live' in ideology by participating in certain practices within specific ideological apparatuses. These practices have definite effects. The brief notes that follow summarize the typical and composite views of lecturers presented to students attending an 'Issues in Education' course at a centre for the training of teachers. On attending the series of lectures given by the 'experts', what did I hear?

I found that the individual is invariably presented in opposition to the group. The entities are always polarized; whilst the individual 'is a unique centre of consciousness', the locus of freedom and choice, the group, on the other hand, is assumed to be coercive and deterministic. The whole of history is then dichotomized into those societies that give priority to the individual and some notion of individual uniqueness, and those societies that stress the primacy of the (authoritarian) group. These categories, the individual and the group, are seen as isolated, static, separate. That the individual and the group could be dialectically related, that, perhaps, we can only have a notion of the individual because of the group, or that it is only through the group that one's potentiality is most realized, is not considered.

After the concepts 'the individual' and 'the group' have been polarized, it is taken for granted that the emphasis should be on the individual. The Kantian notion of respect for persons is usually invoked — the attempt to improve the world must be through the individual, through the actions of a person's moral behaviour. But what about oppression in South Africa? This, too, is seen in moral terms, as a struggle between 'good' and 'evil'. Again the freewill of the individual is emphasized; good and evil stem from individual choices. Conflict is seen as a (regrettable) ethical matter rather than the struggle of economic and class interests. It is conceded that pressure should be exerted against oppressors, but it is asserted that, however great the oppression, revolutionary violence is never justified.

In such a framework it is stressed that the family and the school are vitally important because of their role in the transmission of norms and moral values. Teachers thus bear an awesome responsibility as they are the conscious custodians of culture — 'an enormous treasure' which it is a privilege to pass on. In fact, teachers are paid specifically for the purpose of initiating the young. Students are asked to consider what sort of teachers they would like to be. A teacher like Mr Chips, for example, or Gradgrind, Ursula Brangwyn, Mrs Brodie?[16] Until the recent deepening of the economic crisis the impression was given to students that there was an unlimited choice, and pressures from capital/industry and the state were not seriously examined. Of course this is now gradually changing.

Within such an ideology it is not surprising that the approach adopted to education is a traditional one, where the teacher unquestionably guides the pupils into the shared values of the 'community'. These views are carried over into politics as well. It is assumed that we have satisfactory constitutional arrangements, with a refined — and adequate — system of checks and balances, and these must be continued as a matter of course.

Here we see how individualism is made into an abstraction; how a rigid separation is constructed between the individual and any larger social movements which might give meaning to 'individual' wants and needs. We can see manifestations of this individualism — the notion that individuals have a primary existence and that forms of society are derived from them — in many spheres. In utilitarian ethics, for example, separate individuals calculate the consequences of this or that action which they might undertake. And in classical economics, trade is described in a model which postulates separate individuals who decide, at some time, to enter into economic or commercial relations. I suggest that the concept of the bourgeois individual distorts understanding of our real social relations and dependence on others. The opposition of the abstract categories 'individual' and 'society' is inadequate, because the individual is a social creation born into relationships and, to some extent, determined by them. The ideas mentioned above, the individual as the centre of consciousness, the humanist view of history, the role of the teacher as the custodian of culture, are topics that will be taken up and discussed in subsequent chapters of this book.

Some Criticisms of Althusser

Althusser's theoretical contribution broke the limits of conventional notions of ideology; it confronted the idealist tradition by putting forward a materialist theory of ideology.[17] Althusser thus opened the way for studying the institutions of the bourgeoisie. There is the contradiction that the study of ideology can easily lead to an emphasis on the determinacy of ideas, to idealism and intellectual academicism, but, on the other hand, the stability of capitalism, the incorporation of the working class may be largely due to the strength and penetration of ideology.

Inevitably, Althusser has been attacked by marxists and non-marxists. It has been said that Althusser's work remains trapped within a model of 'levels'. This introduces a metaphor of space and structure, and it entails certain pre-inscribed attributes. Levels must have something that both binds them together *and* holds them apart. Moreover, the concept of 'levels' presupposes the existence of something *a priori*. Others have said that Althusser is trapped in a base-superstructure model, the base being static, the superstructure being dynamic; that the way Althusser writes separates ideology from the levels of production, the material base. The ISA paper, in particular, has been criticized for its functionalism and for its over-determinism. It stressed social reproduction to such an extent that Althusser has been reproached for lacking any notion of class resistance, class struggle.[18] A narrow emphasis on the reproduction thesis has a further limitation. It is static, it neglects the fact that the state-education relation is located in history: it has changed and is changing.

Ironically, the criticisms of Althusser that have had the widest repercussions in Britain have come from those that were his leading adherents. Paul Q. Hirst argues that though Althusser has tried to break with economism, he has not really done so.[19] In the ISA essay, for example, ideology and the state have simple pre-given functions that derive from the economy. Hirst finds the concept of relative autonomy of the levels inadequate; it simply juxtaposes two notions, autonomy and determination, which are logically opposed to each other. He insists that we have to take the distinctiveness of the ideological and political levels (their autonomy) seriously or revert openly to simple economism.

In short, Hirst believes that the concept of relative autonomy is a logical obstruction to scientific analysis, and that political and ideological (signifying) practices must be given a self-determined status free from essentialist taints. With this argument Hirst seems to be making a critique of classical marxism itself, if we take marxism to mean a science of the social formation, based on determination in the last instance by the economic level. It is not necessary to go into Hirst's critique in detail here. My aim now is to focus on the recent bitter and polemical attack against Althusser and his co-workers made by the English historian Edward Thompson from the humanist camp.

Thompson rejects abstract theory, all abstraction and analytical interrogation. He argues that in Althusserian marxism theoretical practice, given an autonomous position, has become theoreticist. Whilst Althusser stresses structure, Thompson sees history as *process*; history is affirmed only as experienced by the agents themselves. Moreover, Thompson believes that the mode of production is not a useful concept. According to Thompson, on the one side there are the historians, who are the guardians of real experience; on the other side are theorists like Althusser, who are interested in ideology and economics. They are guilty of abstractionism, reductionism, vanguardism. Althusser is then accused of being a threat to historical materialism — and of being a Stalinist.[20]

In the chapters that follow I will consider the arguments of these two differing traditions, humanist marxism and structuralist marxism, more closely. To illustrate the debate I will focus on three areas of the school curriculum: history, English literature, and cultural studies. I believe that most students are not made aware of the political and economic context, the structural determinants that influence our lives. I want to suggest that the kind of curriculum which is developed will depend upon our explicit or implicit positions on questions of ontology and epistemology: of what exists in the world and how that world can be known. Our presuppositions about experience and structure influence the form and the content of teaching.

Chapter 2

History, Experience and Structure

In this chapter I will focus on some of the key concepts used in the debate about history between humanist marxists and structuralist marxists. As these theorists hold a wide range of theories, for the purpose of discussion here I will take Althusserianism as representing the structuralist position and the work of the English historian Edward Thompson as representing the humanist viewpoint.

Writers such as Edward Thompson (and Raymond Williams, whose work will be examined in the next chapter) stress the importance of culture and lived experience.[1] One of the chief characteristics of humanist marxism is that it gives priority to agency, the portrayal of experience, and class consciousness. Class consciousness is held to be a mode of handling experiences in cultural terms.

Agency, Experience and Class

What is the part of conscious human choice and initiative in history? What is the role of action and values in the generation of social structures? Thompson states his view clearly; his greatest work *The Making of the English Working Class* begins: 'The working class did not rise like the sun at an appointed time. It was present at its own making.' For this making was an active process, which 'owes as much to agency as to conditioning.' The early English proletariat was not the mere product of the advent of the factory system. On the contrary, 'the working class made itself as much as it was made'.[2] The question of agency is, of course, the argument concerning predetermination and freewill. In the formation of the English working class Thompson stresses agency rather than necessity.

But, as Perry Anderson, a trenchant critic of Thompson, has pointed out, the term 'agent' in everyday usage possesses two opposite connotations; it signifies at once active initiator and passive instrument (for example, agent of a foreign power), and it is very easy for writers to slip from one usage to the other.[3] Moreover, it is difficult to judge statements about proportions of agency and necessity because of the problem of proof: we do not know what would count as a criterion of truth.

Undoubtedly the most fundamental concept for Thompson is experience. The crucial medium in which men and women convert objective determinations into subjective initiatives is experience — the junction between 'being and consciousness'. Experience is not only the lived fabric of society; it is the solution in which 'structure is transmuted into process' and 'the subject re-enters history.' But, again, in ordinary language use there are several meanings which lead to ambiguity. 'Experience' usually denotes an occurrence or episode as it is lived by the participants. But another meaning of 'experience' indicates an alteration of the agent's consciousness so that his actions are modified on a subsequent occasion.[4]

Now, whilst it is admitted that many structuralists, like Althusser, wrongly identify experience with the world of illusion, humanists like Thompson invert the error, identifying experience essentially with insight and learning. Anderson argues that those who stress experience are faced with an insuperable problem: what ensures that a particular experience (of distress or disaster) will inspire a particular cognitively or morally appropriate conclusion? The fact is that self-same events can be lived through by agents who draw diametrically opposed conclusions from them.[5] One has only to consider the disasters which such salient experiences as religious faith or national loyalty have brought upon those in their grip.

I would want to argue that it is quite common for social groups and classes to construct their identity through experiences, which, whilst understandable in empirical terms, cannot be justified morally or politically. For example, sections of the working class have learnt to be racist through their experience, but the social and political consequences are lamentable. The term 'experience' is no guarantee of truth — or goodness.

Thompson has argued vigorously against structural definitions of the proletariat:

> Class happens when some men, as a result of common experiences (inherited or shared), feel and articulate the identity of their interests as between themselves, and as against those whose interests are different from (and usually

opposed to) theirs.... Class is a social and cultural formation which cannot be defined abstractly.... When we speak of a class we are thinking of a very loosely defined body of people who share the same congeries of interests, social experiences, traditions and value-systems, who have a disposition to behave as a class, to define themselves in their actions and in their consciousness in relation to other groups of people in class ways. But class itself is not a thing, it is a happening.[6]

He stresses heavily that the working class is an active historical subject; according to Thompson, it is in the process of struggling that people discover themselves as classes, they come to know the discovery as class consciousness: 'Classes arise because men and women, in determinative productive relations, identify their antagonistic interests, and come to struggle, to think, and to value in class ways.'[7]

I agree with writers like Perry Anderson and Gerry Cohen who contend that Thompson's view of class is far too voluntarist and subjectivist. In Thompson's view it seems that a class is only formed when people develop a consciousness of their common condition and interest. Would this mean that a set of people (bound by similar production relations) that was not (yet) conscious of itself was not a class? It was precisely because of this sort of problem that Marx made the valuable distinction between a 'class in itself', a class that is not conscious of itself, and a 'class for itself', a class conscious of itself in opposition to other classes.

But the main point is this: the whole thrust of Thompson's argument is to detach class from its objective anchorage in determinate relations of production and identify it with subjective consciousness or culture. Cohen argues that an important truth motivates Thompson's misconceived repudiation of the structural idea of class. It is possible to agree with Thompson that production relations do not mechanically determine class consciousness. But it does not follow from this that class may not be defined purely in terms of production relations.

The traditional marxist view is that

a person's class is established by nothing but his objective place in the network of ownership relations, however difficult it may be to identify such places neatly. His consciousness, culture and politics do not enter the *definition* of his class position. Indeed, these exclusions are required to protect the substantive character of the marxian thesis that class position strongly conditions consciousness, culture and politics.[8]

In short, class is an objective relation to means of production, independent of will or attitude.

Marx's Abstract Concepts

Humanists, on the whole, tend to regard abstract concepts with suspicion; but a strength of the structuralist position, it seems to me, is that they recognize their importance, particular emphasis being placed on the mode of production (a concept we will be using in the next chapter) and the contradictions between the forces and the relations of production. For a humanist like Thompson it seems that any focus on the mode of production necessarily denies experience — that which is lived out in culture and consciousness, in feelings and moral values. *He therefore rejects the concept 'mode of production' as not being useful.*

Before examining the concept 'mode of production' let us look at the important role abstraction plays within classical marxism. Marx argued that it was necessary to go beyond appearances, beyond the manner in which social relations are experienced, in order to arrive at knowledge of those social relations. He did not identify the real with the empirical. Appearances, taken at face value, are misleading. They can only be understood in the light of the theory of historical materialism.

Marx held that his work was scientific. Science was the process of producing knowledge by going behind the surface appearance of things to the essence; he wrote that all science would be superfluous if the outward appearance and the essence of things directly coincided. Science has to conceptualize the phenomena underlying appearance; it has to produce concepts which can grasp, appropriate, the hidden phenomena. Its task is to produce knowledge of how the hidden phenomena determine and give rise to the phenomena which are apparent and observable.

Consider the following well-known example: the exchange between capitalist and labourer in which labour power is bought and sold has the appearance of and is experienced as an equal exchange. The labour theory of value uncovers not the 'reality' behind an illusion, but another, deeper level of social relations of production, which explains not only why that exchange is really unequal, but also why it has the form of an equal exchange.

In several recent contributions to the philosophy of social science Althusser's interpretation of Marx is used to establish the thesis that marxism does not identify the real with what·is experienced.[9] The real is a multi-layered structure, consisting of entities and processes lying at different levels of that structure. The empirical world with which we are familiar is on the surface level but is causally connected to 'deeper', ontological levels, and it is by virtue of these causal connections that we can use sense-data, experience and observation in constructing knowledge of the structures and processes of the real. These causal connections cannot themselves be understood through experience, because neither the underlying structures nor the connection between these structures and the empirical world are themselves experienced. The connection can only be reconstructed in knowledge.

The Concept 'Mode of Production'

Let us begin the examination of the concept 'mode of production' by considering the famous statement from Marx's Preface of 1859, in which he summarized the materialist conception of history:

> In the social production of their life, men enter into definite relations that are indispensable and independent of their will, relations of production which correspond to a definite stage of development of their material productive forces. The sum total of these relations of production constitutes the economic structure of society, the real foundation on which rises a legal and political superstructure and to which correspond definite forms of social consciousness. The mode of production of material life conditions the social, political, and intellectual life process in general. It is not the consciousness of men that determines their being, but, on the contrary, their social being that determines their consciousness.[10]

In this Preface Marx espouses the following thesis: (1) the forces of production tend to develop throughout history; they are means of production (raw materials, instruments) and labour power; (2) the relations of production are explained by the level of development of its forces of production. (The relations of production are relationships of ownership or effective control: slave/master, serf/lord, worker/capitalist.) This 'primacy' thesis implies that changes in forces of production bring about changes in relations of production. The

main determinant, the general principle of history, then, is production — but the form in which it operates is specific for each mode of
production. Each mode of production has a specific structure of
relations between production, distribution and exchange.

Marx uses the concept of a *mode of production*, a highly abstract
concept, in several senses; sometimes it refers specifically to production, sometimes to the economic process as a whole, and sometimes
to all social relations, not only the economic and political but the
ideological relations as well. It is in this third sense that the concept is
used in this book.

Now, the society in which we live is a particular social formation; it is not itself a mode of production. In other words, the
capitalist mode of production (CMP) is not the same as the British
social formation; the former is a much more abstract concept than the
latter, which is specific. The capitalist mode of production is defined
by forces of production (means of production plus labour power) and
relations of production. A particular social formation is the articulation of different modes of production. A social formation may not be
a national state but a set of national social formations, or may be
smaller than a national state; it is the product of several modes of
production which may co-exist in one social formation.

Now, in the debate between humanists and structuralists Perry
Anderson has insisted on the importance of these concepts:

> It is, and must be, the dominant *mode of production* that
> confers fundamental unity on a social formation, allocating
> their objective positions to the classes within it, and distribut-
> ing the agents within each class.... Class struggle itself is not
> a causal prius in the sustentation of order, for *classes are
> constituted by modes of production, and not vice versa....*
> Among the most fundamental of all mechanisms of social
> change, according to historical materialism, are the systematic
> contradictions between *forces and relations of production*, not
> just social conflicts between classes generated by antagonistic
> relations of production alone. The former *overlap* with the
> latter because one of the major forces of production is always
> labour, which simultaneously figures as a class specified by
> the relations of production. But they do not coincide. Crises
> within modes of production are not identical with confronta-
> tions between classes. The two may or may not fuse accord-
> ing to the historical occasion.[11]

In sum, mode of production and class struggle are always at work, *but the second must be activated by the first* for it to achieve its determinate effects.

The 'Base-Superstructure' Debate

Another characteristic feature of the bitter polemic between marxist structuralists and humanists is that the latter tend to stress Marx's early (and middle) works, those texts which stress concepts such as alienation. This is usually combined with an omission of, or hostility to, the later 'economic' works, such as *Grundrisse* and *Capital*. Some humanists feel that Marx's work on political economy stresses economic production and therefore denies the relative autonomy of the superstructure. Thompson has said that Marx's narrow concern with economics sets aside the 'many activities and relations (of power, of consciousness, sexual, cultural, normative) which are not the concern of Political Economy, which have been defined out of Political Economy, and for which it has no terms.'[12] In short, humanist marxists, and one could include Raymond Williams here, fear that a stress on concepts like mode of production must lead to economic reductionism.

I want to argue that the humanists' stress on the early and middle works of Marx means that their own work is limited, because in those texts Marx had not yet developed concepts such as the forces and relations of production. Structuralists like Althusser and Balibar rightly tend to emphasize the concept of mode of production because it gives us the means of differentiating one major type of historical structure from another, it enables us to think of the diversity of socio-economic forms. The concept of the contradictions between forces of production and relations of production is absolutely vital for historical materialism as it is the deepest spring of long-term historical change.

What can be said about the charge of economic reductionism that is so often levelled against the structuralists? In fact, the Althusserian concept of social formation was 'initially introduced as a forcible reminder that the diversity of human practices in any society is irreducible to economic practice alone.'[13] The term 'society' was rejected because it had a simplistic connotation; in contrast, the term 'social formation' refers to the economic, political, and ideological levels (instances or practices) and the need for specific historical accounts for each. Of the humanists' deep suspicion of a society with different 'levels' Anderson has stated: 'It is the misgiving that to

distinguish analytically between various instances in a social formation tends to induce the belief that these exist substantively as
separate objects, physically divisible from each other in the real
world.'[14]

On Althusser's behalf it could be said that he has always stressed
the strictly metaphorical nature of the base/superstructure distinction, and the distinction between the object of knowledge and the real
object. It should also be noted that the main contributions of
Althusserian theory have not been in economic determinants at all
but in ideology. Indeed, the main concern of Althusser has been the
structuring of thought and consciousness through ideological
processes.[15] He has repeatedly emphasized the irreducibility, the
'effectivity', and the 'materiality' of ideology.

The Teaching of History

What is the relevance for teachers of the above discussion? I believe
that in most of our schools and colleges history is still taught with an
emphasis on great individuals. There is a lack of theoretical founda-
tion; indeed, there is often a hostility to theory, which is seen in
opposition to empirical scholarship. Even at university level the
problematic and philosophical character of historical inquiry is rarely
discussed.

My contention is that an understanding of these debates is
crucial to what (and how) we teach. Socialist teachers are faced with
the following dilemma: Should the teaching of history, for example,
be underpinned by a humanist or a structuralist approach? Both can
be (but need not necessarily be) marxist. If humanist marxism were
accepted as the basis of the teaching of history, what would be the
main characteristics of such an approach? As suggested earlier,
humanism is best understood as an outlook which opposes all
deterministic, mechanical or functionalist accounts of the social
world. Humanism rejects all approaches to history in which lived
relations are marginalized or where there is a use of abstractions or
abstract typologies. It repudiates rationalism and conceptual 'aprior-
ism' (the notion that there exists the possibility of genuine knowledge
independent of experience) and insists on getting inside the minds,
feelings, and rationalities of the historical agents themselves.

The curriculum of the humanist marxists would emphasize
classes as historical agents; it would be argued that classes, present at
their own making, are forged in struggle. The stress would be on the

activist elements, the 'class for itself'. Moreover, it is the *quality* of human relationships within the class that would be regarded as important rather than the actual structuring of the relations. In short, humanists would argue against the base/superstructure formulation, which is seen as vulgar economism. Reacting against the tendency to empty the 'superstructure' of any real material force, they would emphasize the role of culture, values, ideas in the school curriculum.

What criticism could be made of such an approach to the teaching of history and the social sciences? The main objection is that, because of the emphasis of the humanists on culture, there could be a persistent neglect in their teaching of the particular character and force of economic relations. It seems that the stress on culture involves vacating the ground of economic relations, and this necessarily leads to an impoverishment of analysis.[16]

Moreover, the stress on the privilege of experience leads to an underdeveloped theoretical enterprise and a tendency to avoid abstract or generalizing discourse. There is a tendency to reject analytical distinctions as a matter of principle. But distinctions are the vital *means* with which we attempt to grasp the 'total social process'. Systematic knowledge and the search for more adequate explanations of social processes require developed analytical procedures.

To summarize, the Althusserian structuralist approach asserts that the implicit trust in the authentic experience of the agent leads to a tendency to ignore external determinations. Secondly, humanists tend to reject the process of systematic self-conscious abstraction that Marx developed. Thirdly, humanists do not sufficiently recognize that social relations are structured, that they have a tendency or force of their own and operate, in part, 'behind our backs'.

It is interesting to speculate on the possible effects of teaching history to students using the humanist approach. Would the humanist stress on the potential of human agency, the power of consciousness to shape collective conditions, help to bring such conditions about? How (and in what ways) would children learn that the humanist approach does not take material conditions sufficiently seriously? On the other hand, teachers using the structuralist approach would present history in a much more deterministic manner. Would their stress on the overpowering weight of structural necessity influence the students to adopt a passive role?

My contention is that an understanding of these debates is crucial to what (and how) we teach. I feel that as teachers we must be more aware of the implications and consequences of the traditions we tacitly accept and promote. The teaching of history would be much improved if students and teachers were systematically introduced to these debates and to a study of structuralism which necessarily focusses on some of the main problems of historiography. But one qualification must be made — there is the danger of over-simplification; humanism and structuralism are not homogeneous, monolithic categories. There are many structuralisms: liberal-academic and marxist. Even within Althusserian structuralism there are many contributory traditions, discourses: the linguistics of Saussure, the structural anthropology of Lévi-Strauss, Lacan's rereading of psychoanalysis, Gramsci's writings on state and civil society. There will be a discussion of all these topics in the chapters that follow. But before we turn our attention to these matters, let us look at the humanist-structuralist debate in relation to literature.

Chapter 3

Literature, Ideology and Schooling

In the previous chapter I discussed some of the issues in the debate between humanist marxism and structuralist marxism concerning the nature of history. In this chapter the debate will be continued, but the focus will be on literature. First there will be a review of the early work of Raymond Williams, a leading representative of the humanist approach. I will then outline one of the new perspectives that are being developed by Terry Eagleton and others, which adopts structuralist marxism as a method for studying literature. It is suggested that the categories Eagleton has proposed could usefully be applied to the study of education. Finally I will relate this debate to the place and function of literature in the educational apparatus.

The Socialist Humanism of Raymond Williams

The greatest figure in literary criticism and cultural studies in Britain today is undoubtedly Raymond Williams, whose achievement has been compared with that of Lukács, Goldmann or Benjamin. His work can be divided, broadly, into three phases; in what follows comment will be made on the first and second phases in order to bring out the humanistic characteristics of his work.

Terry Eagleton tells us that when Williams came to writing in the 1950s, the criticism of the 1930s, compounded as it was of vulgar marxism, bourgeois empiricism, and romantic idealism, could yield him almost nothing.[1] Like Christopher Caudwell, Williams was severely deprived of the theoretical materials from which to construct a socialist criticism. Intellectually isolated, what he did he did almost single-handedly.

One of the main formative influences on his early development was F.R. Leavis' journal *Scrutiny*.[2] This journal contended that 'human values' were being brutally overridden by the development of contemporary capitalism. Driven back to the 'artisanal' images of a pre-capitalist past, the journal's obsolescent and idealist solution was the organic community of a mythicized English past. Williams rejected *Scrutiny*'s position, because he realized it was fundamentally anti-democratic and élitist. At this time he also rejected marxism, because 'there was, in this position, a polarization and abstraction of economic life on the one hand and culture on the other, which did not seem to me to correspond to the social experience of culture as others had lived it, and as one was trying to live it oneself.'[3]

Though Williams rejected the political position of *Scrutiny*, he was greatly influenced by it. *Scrutiny*'s insistence on community, tradition, moral value, and the centrality of the 'lived' provided the terms through which questions of personal identity could be explored and politically generalized. Williams' insistence on lived experience, clearly expressed in the above quotation, is a key feature throughout his work. He continually offers his own experience as historically representative and socially typical. Not surprisingly, Williams' early work has been called 'Left-Leavisite'.

Later, in the second phase, Williams seeks to extend and connect what is still in many ways a Leavisian perspective to a 'socialist humanism'. In *Culture and Society* he took the romantic 'radical-conservative' lineage of nineteenth-century England and extracted from it those 'radical' elements which could be grafted on to a 'socialist humanism': tradition, community, organicism, growth, wholeness. Terry Eagleton has suggested that Williams did not realize the reactionary character of the tradition with which he was dealing, and that what *Culture and Society* did was to consecrate the reformism of the labour movement. The book

> tended to a dangerous conflation of productive modes, social relations, ethical, political, and aesthetic ideologies, collapsing them into the empty anthropological abstraction of 'culture'. Such a collapsing not only abolishes any hierarchy of actual priorities, reducing the social formation to a 'circular' Hegelian totality and striking political strategy dead at birth, but inevitably *over-subjectivises* that formation.[4]

These are, of course, all the characteristics one associates with the humanist problematic.

Williams' *The Long Revolution*, besides containing organicist aesthetics and corporatist sociology, also contains an idealist epistemology. The root of all three was a form of romantic populism. His political gradualism rests on a deep-seated trust in the capacity of individuals to create 'new meanings and values'. There is no doubt that Williams has a generous reverence for human capacities. What Williams is stressing in his early work is that people do in fact create their meanings and values in common, but this common process is then blocked by capitalist imposition. In this work there is often a contradiction: on the one hand he opposes capitalist domination, and yet on the other hand he has simultaneously to deny it, because not to do so would suggest that ordinary people were not, after all, the true creators of meanings and values.

Much of Williams' work is permeated by a suspicion of the economic level and its determining role. He is, for example, highly critical of the notion of base and superstructure 'with its suggestion of a fixed and definite spatial relationship'. In his view orthodox marxists began to think of the base and the superstructure as if they were separable concrete entities. 'In doing so they lost sight of the very processes — not abstract relations but constitutive processes — which it should have been the special function of historical material-ism to emphasize.'[5] In other words, Williams argues, there is a ten-dency for analytic categories to become substantive descriptions which then take habitual priority over the whole social process.

Williams, like Thompson, rejects the Althusserian formulation of economic, political and ideological levels because any such distinc-tion is a false abstraction — it distinguishes analytically things which always appear connected in any historical example or in 'experience'. But if the economic, political and ideological all interact and affect each other, then the problem of determinism is evaded and we are led to a form of relativism.

In Williams' *early* work there are several misconceptions about the structures of advanced capitalist formations. His misunderstand-ing of the nature of class and power is evident in his famous definition of culture, 'the study of relations between elements in a whole way of life'. This view ignores the role of ideology and neglects consideration of power:

> There is not a special class, or group of men, who are involved
> in the creation of meanings and values.... Such creation
> could not be reserved to a minority, however gifted, and [is]
> not, even in practice, so reserved: the meanings of a particular
> form of life of a people, at a particular time, seem to come
> from the whole of their common experience.[6]

Williams is naively wrong here — there are indeed such classes and groups who effectively define the meanings and values of common experience in their own class terms for others.

Another feature of Williams' thought is an antagonism towards abstraction. For example, there is his well-known rejection of the concept of 'masses': 'There are in fact no masses: there are only ways of seeing people as masses.'[7] On this statement Eagleton comments: 'In thus defending "people" against what he sees as a cynically manipulative abstraction, Williams traded a theoretical instrument of revolutionary struggle for the short change of liberal humanitarianism.'[8] Williams insists that men and women really are unique individuals, but he does not realize that they must mass and fight to achieve their full individual humanity. The massing together of individuals is a material condition of their political emancipation.

To summarize, it has been suggested that Williams' early work has the following characteristics. Firstly, there is the stress on lived experience. Reasoning, unless it springs organically from lived experience, is likely to be suspect. Secondly, he is wary of abstraction; in fact, it has been said that his work betrays a muted strain of anti-intellectualism. He has, for example, a deep suspicion of economics and of any view of culture which stresses the role of the economic 'base'.[9] Thirdly, Williams' residual populism, as Eagleton has commented, is at the roots of consistent *over-subjectivizing of the social formation*. Williams resembles the young Lukács, it seems to me, not only in his theoretical idealism, but in the fact that he is highly critical of any 'reflectionist' theory of art.[10] However, it must be remembered that at the time Williams started writing there was an absence of mass working-class struggle. The *idealist* bent of his political conceptions was the effect of the divorce of social democrats in the Labour Party from the working class.

It should be stressed that the above remarks refer only to Williams' early work. He has now surpassed the gradualism of the 'middle' phase. The earlier idealist hostility to the dominance of material over mental production is being progressively modified.[11] *The Country and the City* is the first of his texts which is actually based on, and uses, marxist concepts. In his most recent work Williams seems to have discovered, via the work of Goldmann and Lukács, a more direct and sympathetic route between his own thinking and the marxist revolutionary tradition.

In the above section it has been pointed out that the early work of Williams in literary and social criticism has the same characteristics as Edward Thompson's work in history.[12] Now, my contention is that if a teacher teaches from a humanist perspective, s/he would stress the importance of lived experience, the capacity of people to create their own meanings and values (a form of voluntarism), and to objectivize the social formation. These idealist tendencies lead to a study of literature and culture without a materialist theory of the social formation. Teaching with such an approach could only mean that students would remain within a humanistic problematic, without an understanding of the relationship between modes of production, ideologies and cultural artifacts.

The Structuralist Marxism of Terry Eagleton

In their studies of literature Lukács, Adorno, Marcuse, Goldmann, and Sartre all accept the problems of traditional aesthetics.[13] It is now being increasingly felt that to incorporate the concerns of aesthetics into marxist criticism is thus necessarily to import into it a set of problems which can only be conceived in idealist terms. And so it could be said that the above writers failed to produce a *new* set of questions which could supplant the concerns of pre-marxist aesthetics. In short, a historical materialist theory of the production of different forms of writing demands a prior break with the concerns of bourgeois aesthetics.

In recent years attempts have been made by Pierre Macherey, Terry Eagleton and others to dislocate criticism from the concerns of idealist bourgeois aesthetics. Macherey, for example, has remarked that 'What is literature?' is a false question, because it is a question which already contains an answer. It implies that literature exists as an eternal and unchangeable thing with an essence. For Macherey the proposition that the writer or artist is a *creator* belongs to humanist ideology. The work is not created by an intention, it is *produced* under determinate conditions, works are produced by a real labour of production. 'All considerations of genius, of the subjectivity of the artist, of his soul, are *on principle* uninteresting.'[14] He suggests that literature should be seen as a *historical* and not an aesthetic category. In particular historical periods literature exists in different forms; what needs to be studied is the difference between these forms. Literature with a capital 'L' does not exist.

Pierre Macherey and Terry Eagleton have both been engaged in a process of *working through* Althusser to produce a new set of concerns which goes beyond those embodied in his work. Eagleton has inflected Brecht's and Benjamin's views on literature through a reading of Althusser and Macherey. This has enabled him to develop a detailed system of concepts which will enable literary production to be explained in materialist terms. It is worth outlining his conception at some length in order to illustrate recent developments in the study of literature and culture.

Eagleton has proposed a critical *method* which integrates structuralist marxism with certain semiological findings. Here I will focus on his presentation of the basic categories, the major constituents, of a marxist theory of literature.[15] They can be listed as follows:

1 General Mode of Production (GMP);
2 Literary Mode of Production (LMP);
3 General Ideology (GI);
4 Authorial Ideology (AuI);
5 Aesthetic Ideology (AI);
6 Text.

Let us now consider these elements, because it is the complex historical articulations of these structures which produce literary texts.

1 General Mode of Production

A mode of production may be characterized as a unity of certain forces and social relations of material production.

2 Literary Mode of Production

In any literate society there will normally exist a number of distinct modes of literary production (poetry, drama, the novel), one of which will be normally dominant. These distinct LMPs are mutually articulated in varying relations of homology, conflict and contradiction. Every LMP is constituted by structures of production, distribution, exchange and consumption. Production presupposes a producer or set of producers, materials, instruments, techniques of production, and the product itself. The forces of literary production consist of labour power organized in certain 'relations of production' (printers, publishers, etc.) to certain materials of production by means of certain determinate productive instruments. The task is to analyze the complex articulations of various LMPs with the general mode of production of a social formation.

What are the relations between the LMP and the GMP? They are dialectical. The forces of production of the LMP are naturally provided by the GMP itself, of which the LMP is a particular substructure. The LMP represents a specific division of labour, determined by the character and stage of development of the GMP, becoming more specialized and diverse as the GMP develops. In developed capitalist social formations the most significant relation of LMP to GMP is that of the LMPs function in the reproduction and expansion of the general mode of production.

3 General Ideology

The GMP always produces a dominant ideological formation which is constituted by a relatively coherent set of 'discourses' of values, representations and beliefs. The term 'general ideology' is used to distinguish it from that specific region within it known as the aesthetic region (or 'aesthetic ideology').

GI typically contains certain general elements or structures — the linguistic, the political and the cultural — which influence the character of the LMP. Consider language: a literary text is related to GI not only by how it deploys language, but by the particular language it uses. Eagleton writes that 'language is a terrain scarred by the cataclysms of political history, strewn with the relics of imperialist, nationalist, regionalist and class combat.... Literature is an agent as well as effect of such struggles.'[16]

There is no necessary homology between GI and LMP. Works belonging to alternative literary modes of production may inhabit the same ideology. Conversely, the same LMP may reproduce mutually antagonistic ideological formations (the fiction of Defoe and Fielding). Moreover, an LMP which reproduces the social relations of the GMP may conflict with some of its dominant ideological modes. (For example, the romantic dissent from bourgeois values and relations is in part determined by the very integration of the LMP into general commodity production.) Conversely, a LMP in conflict with GMP social relations may, nevertheless, reproduce its dominant ideological forms.

4 Authorial Ideology

By 'authorial ideology' is meant the author's biography; social class, sex, nationality, religion are some of the factors which must be considered here. AuI should never be treated in isolation from GI, but must be studied in its articulation with it. Between GI and AuI relations of effective homology, partial disjunction and severe contradiction are possible.

A GMP produces a GI which contributes to reproducing it; it also produces a (dominant) LMP which in general reproduces, and is reproduced by, the GMP, but which also reproduces, and is reproduced by, the GI.

5 Aesthetic Ideology

Aesthetic ideology is the specific aesthetic region of GI articulated with other such regions (the ethical, religious, etc.). AI is an internally complex formation including a number of subsectors, of which the literary is one. This literary subsector is itself internally complex and is constituted by a number of levels: theories of literature, critical practices, literary traditions, *genres*.

The forces and relations of literary production, on the basis of their determination by the GMP, produce the possibility of certain distinct literary *genres*. The novel, for example, can be produced only at a certain stage of development of a LMP, but whether this potential is historically activated is determined not by the LMP alone, but by its conjuncture with GI and AI. What forms and *genres* are actually selected for development may be dictated by what exists already — dictated, that is, by AI on the basis of GI. Conversely, the concept of and 'need for' a new form may develop relatively autonomously within aesthetic ideology, and a LMP modified or transformed to produce it.

It should be noted that an author may produce progressive texts using outmoded forms within an obsolescent LMP (William Morris), or may produce ideologically conservative texts within a historically progressive LMP (Henry Fielding). It is a question in each case of specifying the precise relations between LMP, GI and AI.

6 The Text

The literary text is produced by an interaction of the structures outlined schematically above. But what is the relation of the text to ideology? The literary text is not the 'expression' of ideology. Eagleton uses the analogy of a dramatic production. A dramatic production does not 'express', 'reflect' or 'reproduce' the dramatic text on which it is based; it 'produces' the text. The relation between text and production is a relation of *labour*: the theatrical instruments (staging, acting skills, etc.) transform the 'raw materials' of the text into a specific product. Another useful analogy is that between ideology in the text and the analysis of dreams, to which we now turn.

Ideology in the Text and the Analysis of Dreams

Freud argued that the analyst must penetrate the manifest content of the dream to uncover its latent content. The analyst's task is not only to lay bare the meaning of a distorted text, but to expose the meaning of the text distortion itself. The truth of the dream lies precisely in its distortion. Psychoanalysis (aspects of this theory will be discussed in chapter 6) reconstructs the actual process of production of the dream.

It could be said that the 'uppermost dream layer' exists to systematize the dream, fill in its gaps, and smooth over its contradictions. But beneath this lies the real, mutilated text of the dream itself, which resists interpretation. The dream, as a distorted and mutilated text, is a conflict and compromise between unconscious material seeking expression and the intervention of an ideological censor. The typical consequence of this is that the unconscious is able to say what it wants, but not in the way it wanted to say it.

Pierre Macherey, who has greatly influenced the work of Terry Eagleton, has stressed the point that the task of criticism and dream analysis is to examine the lacunae and hiatuses (the gaps and pauses), the distortion mechanisms which produce that ruptured discourse. He argues, in short, that we should study the unconscious — not of the author, but of the work. The unconscious of the work is constructed in the moment of its entry into literary form, in the gap between the project and the formulation. He suggests that we study the splitting within the work, the division in its unconscious.

For Macherey the task of criticism is to establish the 'unspoken' in the text. We should ask of every work what it tacitly implies. The explicit requires the implicit; for in order to say anything there are other things which must not be said.[17] Meaning, then, is the relation between the implicit and the explicit. What is important in the work is what it cannot say; and so Macherey suggests that we investigate the silences, the absences. The text is, as it were, ideologically forbidden to say certain things. In trying to tell the truth authors find themselves forced to the limits of the ideology within which they write.

Because a text contains gaps and silences it is always incomplete; it is not a rounded, coherent whole. In fact, there is no central unity or essence to it, just continuous conflict and contradictions of meanings. The task of the critic is to seek out the principle of its conflict of meaning. The critic, then, is not a therapist of the text, his/her task is not to cure or complete it, but to explain why it is as it is.

Some Categories for an Analysis of Education

I now want to suggest that the categories which Eagleton has proposed could perhaps be adapted and applied to theorize regarding the educational apparatus. I believe that the study of structures similar to the ones outlined could provide useful accounts of different types of education. Of course, a considerable amount of research would need to be done to analyze adequately the complex interconnections between various educational modes of production and the GMP.

By *Educational Modes of Production* (EMP) I mean the variety of social forms and institutions in which the production and consumption of education is organized and carried out. In advanced industrial societies there are a number of distinct educational modes of production, some of which are dominant. There are different types of schools in the state, the independent (private), and the 'religious' sectors. At the tertiary level there are colleges of further education, institutes of higher education, polytechnics, universities. An important question to note here is: how does one decide that any two institutions are examples of distinct educational modes of production as opposed to variations of one educational mode of production?

Every educational mode of production is constituted by structures of production, distribution, exchange and consumption. The consumption of education is based largely on class lines. Most middle-class parents choose schools for their children which provide a qualitatively different experience of education than that received by working-class pupils.

Obviously, we need to specify the actual productive process in the different institutions to identify what is meant by 'the educational mode of production'. Production presupposes a set of *producers*, the application of labour power (by teachers, heads of departments, head teachers, ect.); the *materials* of production are the commonsense knowledge and skills, the culture with which children enter the school. On the other hand, there is also the knowledge and skills which teachers and/or the school system think it necessary or desirable to transmit. Then there are the instruments and *techniques* of production (timetabling, all the work within the classroom: teaching, marking, the use of textbooks, etc.) and the *product*: the socialized individual.

At times there may be a disjunction between historically co-existent educational modes of production. For example, there may be types of schooling that are historical survivals from a previous mode of production. Similarly there may be schools that pre-figure the forms and social relations of a future socialist society.

The relations between the educational mode of production and the general mode of production are dialectical. It could be said that on the whole the educational mode of production is determined by the character and stage of the general mode of production, becoming more centralized, diverse, specialized, and working on pupils for a longer period of time as the general mode of production develops.[18] At all times the GMP bears upon the EMP to exclude certain social groups (black people, women) and the working class from certain elements of educational production and consumption. The EMP's main function is the reproduction of the social relations of the general mode of production, which is, in the last instance, the main determinant.

General Ideology (GI) typically contains structures like the linguistic, the political, and the cultural which influence the character of the educational modes of production. There is no necessary homology (correspondence in structure or development) between GI and EMP. Schools belonging to alternative education modes of production (say, public schools and free schools) may propagate the same ideology. Conversely, the same educational modes of production or forms of schooling may reproduce different or antagonistic forms of ideology (for example, Roedean and Dartington Hall). An EMP which reproduces the social relations of the GMP may conflict with some of its ideological modes. On the other hand, an EMP in conflict with GMP social relations may nevertheless reproduce its dominant ideological forms. This seems to be the case with many 'progressive schools'.

Whilst schools in the state sector prepare the majority of pupils for their roles in the workforce, schools in the independent (private) sector provide the socialization of the political élite. As is well known, the ruling classes receive their training — with its stress on self-confidence and leadership — largely in public schools and the older, more prestigious universities.[19] General Ideology, then, permeates *all* schools. The curriculum, in my view, is a selective representation, a structuring, of General Ideology.

Teachers' (personal) Ideology (TI) consists of many important biographical factors, such as the teacher's social class, sex, race, etc., which infleunce the educational apparatus at the level of administration, teaching in the classroom, the form and content of educational materials, the overt and the 'hidden' curriculum. Between GI and TI there may be relations of effective homology, partial disjunction or severe contradiction. I will discuss the problem of teachers' social class and their educational practice in chapter 9.

Pedagogic Ideology (PI) is a specific educational region of General Ideology and has many levels. It includes occupational and professional ideologies, theories of education, teaching styles, 'child development', theories of learning, decisions as to how children should be taught (that is to say, in mixed ability groups or streaming, etc.). It could be argued that the forces and relations of educational production, on the basis of their determination by the GMP, produce the possibility of certain distinct teaching styles and methods. Child-centred teaching, for example, can arise only at a certain stage of development of an EMP. The type of teaching styles favoured at different times and places may be dictated by many factors. How and why a new form of teaching may develop relatively autonomously within PI and an EMP is modified or transformed to produce it, will have to be a matter for future research.

It is often the case that teachers transmit progressive ideas using outmoded forms and techniques. (It has been said that this was Gramsci's contention and practice — an issue that will be explored in chapter 10). On the other hand, there are also teachers who adopt progressive forms, but the content of what they teach is ideologically conservative. Another element within PI that needs to be examined is the influence of writers on education. What were the effects on pedagogy, for example, of the 'Black Papers'?

Finally, we come to the product: the 'socialized' individual. The recipient of knowledge, the learner, too frequently remains a cypher, assumed and untheorized. I suggest that the socialized individual is produced by an interaction of the structures outlined schematically above. But this is *not* to say that the learner is a mere effect of the teaching process. Though the EMP 'produces' the individual, that does not mean that the latter is a *tabula rasa* or a passive object. There is a sense in which materials limit the type of production process to which they can be subjected. That is to say, the product is the result of the *interaction* of the attempt to produce and the refractoriness of any material. The individual has its own class, gender and race interests which may coincide or conflict with the varying ideologies of teachers and schooling. Students may reject the knowledge presented by the school or they may consume and internalize it. Much depends on the influence of social class, the family, the peer group, the school itself, and other factors.

I think a marxist sociology of education must allow for the possibility of various student responses to schooling and not see it as some sort of monolithic indoctrination. Students are not merely 'produced', but are also the product of their own labour. Individuals, to some extent, produce their own texts. Socialization is never completely successful. There are always gaps, possibilities, spaces in which to resist bourgeois hegemony. We have now come full circle, because this is the main theme of the last few chapters: the relationship between voluntarism and determinism.

To conclude this section I want to reiterate that a General Mode of Production produces a General Ideology which contributes to reproducing it; it also produces a dominant Educational Mode of Production, which in general reproduces, and is reproduced by, the General Mode of Production, but which also produces, and is reproduced by, the General Ideology. It would seem to me that Althusser (ideology), Bernstein (language) and Bourdieu (culture) in their different ways are exploring just these relationships in their theories of social reproduction. The work of Bowles and Gintis on schooling in the United States is a concrete example of an empirical study which also stresses the role of education in the expansion and reproduction of the General Mode of Production.[20]

Literature and Schooling

The classical marxist emphasis on the function which ideology performs in reproducing the conditions and relations necessary to the capitalist mode of production is also expressed in the studies by Renée Balibar.[21] Focussing on the use of literary texts within the French educational system, she argues that the description of certain texts as 'literary' and their restricted use within certain types of schools was a manifestation of class struggle in the sphere of language.

What was the tactic by which the bourgeoisie created and

reproduced for itself a position of supremacy in language? In the second half of the nineteenth century the national education system split along class lines between its primary and secondary levels. In the primary schools working-class children were taught grammar mechanically; they simply received the rules and were offered no understanding of their genesis or of the logic underlying them. The study of these was reserved for the secondary schools, populated largely by the children of the bourgeoisie, and was developed chiefly through the study of comparative grammar on the basis of selected 'literary' texts.

The result is that the bourgeoisie experiences language as its own. The subordinate classes, by contrast, experience the language as a realm from which they are excluded. This is an example of how literary texts serve to maintain bourgeois dominance in language. According to Balibar, literary practice constitutes an essentially ideological operation in its attempts to heal or placate class and ideological contradictions inscribed within language itself. Literature exists not as an absolute, 'out there', but as a constructed element within a specific ideological apparatus — education — where it both legitimates and disguises the reproduction of linguistic inequality.

I would contend that the uses to which literary texts have been put within the educational system in Britain have also been concerned to reinforce a class differentiation at the level of language. Through their grip on examination boards and their control over the training of teachers, the literature departments of our universities effectively determine both *what* literature should be taught and *how* it should be taught.[22]

In a recent work Raymond Williams has reminded us that 'education' is a selection and organization from all available social knowledge at a particular time. He calls it the 'selective tradition'; it is

> that which, within the terms of an effective dominant culture, is always passed off as 'the tradition', '*the* significant past'. But always selectivity is the point; the way in which from a whole possible area of past and present, certain meanings and practices are chosen for emphasis, certain other meanings and practices are neglected and excluded. Even more crucially, some of the meanings are reinterpreted, diluted, or put into forms which support or at least do not contradict other elements within the effective dominant culture. The process of education..., the family, the practical definitions and organization of work, the selective tradition at an intellectual

and theoretical level: all these forces are involved in a continual making and remaking of an effective dominant culture.[23]

It follows from this that we should always be asking: Whose knowledge is it? Who selected it? Why is it organized and taught in this way? In whose interest is this particular form of knowledge (facts, skills, propensities and dispositions) taught?

We may now draw some conclusions about the place and function of literature in schools. It is important that we should consider the teaching of literature in the educational apparatus for the following reasons. First, literature is a crucial mechanism by which the language and ideology of an imperialist class establishes its hegemony. But it is also a means by which a subordinated class, region or state can preserve at the ideological level a historical identity eroded at the political. Secondly, it is vital to study not only the process of production and consumption of literary texts, but the *function* of such production: its contribution to the reproduction of the social relations of the mode of production. Thirdly, literature has been institutionalized: certain texts are severed from their social formations, defined as 'literary', graded and ranked, constituted into literary traditions, and interrogated to yield a set of ideologically presupposed responses. From the infant school to the university faculty, literature has become an instrument for the insertion of individuals into the forms of the dominant ideology. The educational apparatus is being forced to have an expanding role in the reproduction of capitalist conditions of existence, that is to say, the knowledge, skills and attitudes necessary for the production of value. Term by term, year by year, schools try to habituate young people to patterns of the dominant culture and to the needs of capital.

In this chapter it has been suggested that some approaches within structuralist marxism can play a valuable part in the understanding of literature. (The contribution of *structuralism* to our knowledge of literature and cultural studies will be examined in the next chapter.) According to Macherey and Eagleton, ideology is held to be the binding force of the social formation, and 'experience' to be the most common form of ideology — it is where the deep structures of the society actually reproduce themselves as conscious life. It has been argued that literature is inescapably ideological. However, because of its relative autonomy it is a practice in which ideology can both exist and be questioned. And so the main value of literature is that it is one of the areas where the grip of ideology can be loosened.

Chapter 4

Structuralism, Literature and Cultural Studies

In the first part of this book I looked at some aspects of marxism; in this part the focus will be on structuralism, those theories based on the pioneering work of Saussure on language. Saussurean structural linguistics first provided the methodological impetus to treat other systems of phenomena as 'languages'. Since the Second World War French structuralism has had an extraordinary impact on social and political thought. Though structuralism constitutes not a unified theory, but a complex network of writings interacting in various ways, there is one core feature: its rejection of the ego.

Not only does structural analysis abandon the search for external causes, it refuses to make the thinking subject an explanatory cause. The work of Lévi-Strauss, Barthes, Lacan, and Foucault (along with the texts of Saussure, Freud and Nietzsche which they use) has called into question the notion of the self as subject or consciousness which might serve as a source of meaning and a principle of explanation. In other words, the researches of psychoanalysis, of linguistics, of anthropology have 'decentred the subject' in relation to the laws of its desire, the forms of its language, the rules of its actions.

The dominant tradition has taken the self as a conscious subject. But once meaning is explained in terms of systems which may escape the grasp of the conscious subject, the self can no longer be identified with consciousness. And as it is displaced from its function as centre or source, the self comes to appear more and more as a construct.

Structuralism

Structuralism is a *method* whose scope includes all human phenomena, embracing not only the social sciences (anthropology, sociology, psychology, politics, economics) but also the humanities (literature, history, linguistics) and the fine arts. It is concerned with the perception and description of structures, which it seeks not on the surface, at the level of the observed, but below or behind empirical reality. What the empirical observer sees is not the structure, but simply the evidence and product of the structure. Just as native speakers of a language have no need of a knowledge of the structure of their own tongue in order to be able to use it, so we should not expect the members of a society to be conscious of its structures, but only to be aware of the concrete manifestations of those structures. Social structures, then, cannot be directly observed but must be deductively constituted.

Structuralism insists that the world does not consist of independently existing objects; the real nature of things may be said to lie not in things themselves, but in the *relationships* which we construct, and then perceive, between them. The full significance of any entity cannot be perceived unless and until it is integrated into the structure of which it forms a part.[1] Structure can be observed in an arrangement of entities which embodies three fundamental ideas:

(1) the idea of wholeness. By wholeness is meant the sense of internal coherence. The constituent parts of the structure conform to a set of intrinsic laws which determine its nature;

(2) the idea of transformation. The structure is not static. The laws which govern it act so as to make it not only structured but structuring. The structure must be capable of transformational procedures whereby new material is constantly processed, capable of generating new aspects of itself;

(3) the idea of self-regulation. The structure is self-regulating in the sense that it makes no appeals beyond itself in order to validate its transformational procedures.

Structures of Language: Ferdinand de Saussure

The central concepts of structuralism were developed in the study of linguistics and anthropology. Ferdinand de Saussure, the Swiss linguist, insisted that language should be studied not only in terms of its individual parts, but in the relationship between these parts, and not only diachronically (over time, historically), but synchronically (at the same time), that is, in terms of its current use and adequacy.[2]

He made a dialectical distinction between *langue* and *parole*. *Langue* refers to the rules and conventions of language; *parole* refers to speech, the individual utterances made by speakers in concrete situations. Saussure made the analogy between the abstract rules called 'chess' and the concrete games of chess played by people in the real world. The rules of chess can be said to exist above and beyond each individual game, and yet they only acquire concrete form in the relationships that develop between the pieces in individual games. So with language. The nature of the *langue* lies beyond, and determines, the nature of each manifestation of *parole*. This is rather like Noam Chomsky's account of the system of 'competence' that must precede and generate individual 'performance'. The *langue* has no concrete existence of its own apart from its manifestation in speech. *Parole* is a small part of the iceberg that appears above the water, *langue* is the larger mass that supports it and is implied by it both in speaker and hearer, but which never itself appears.

Another distinction Saussure made was that between signifier and signified. The sound image made by the word 'apple' is the signifier, and the *concept* of an apple is the signified. The structural relationship between the signifier and the signified constitutes a linguistic sign, and a language is made up of these. Now, the linguistic sign is *arbitrary*; this means that it stands for something by convention and common usage, not by necessity. There is no necessary connection between the word 'apple' and the idea 'apple'; in France, for instance, the word for apple is 'pomme'.

Signs are defined by their difference from each other in the network of signs which is the signifying system. Saussure argues that languages divide or articulate the world in different ways. The world, which without signification would be experienced as a continuum, is divided up by language into entities which then readily come to be experienced as distinct. Language, in short, makes the world intelligible by differentiating between concepts. In learning its native language, the child learns a set of differentiating concepts which identify not given entities but socially constructed signified. Language in an important sense speaks us.

Structures in Anthropology: Lévi-Strauss

American structural linguistics, closely linked with anthropology, focused on the relationship between language and the cultural 'setting' in which it occurred. Edward Sapir and later Benjamin Lee

Whorf believed that the 'shape' of a culture was in fact determined by, or at any rate clearly 'structured' in the same way as, that culture's language:

> The worlds in which different societies live are distinct worlds, not merely the same world with different labels attached.... We see and hear and otherwise experience very largely as we do because the language habits of our community predispose certain choices of interpretation.[3]

The assumption, then, is not that reality itself is relative but that different aspects of it are noticed by, or presented to, us. None of us can claim access to uncoded, 'pure' or objective experience of a 'real', permanently existing world.

I alluded to the concepts synchrony and diachrony. The synchronic is the dimension of the instantaneous, atemporal and unchanging, the systematic, holistic and functional. The diachronic is the temporal dimension, the dimension of the succession of moments, of the passage of time, of change, evolution, decay and re-growth. In the synchronic, time does not pass and information does not degrade. All processes are reversible. In the diachronic, disorder (entropy) tends to increase, processes cannot usually be reversed, and there is a directional element present which is lacking in the synchronic.

As I mentioned earlier, Saussure made the distinction between a collective, systematic structure on the one hand — the *langue* — and an individual, articulated speech, or *parole*, on the other. Roman Jakobson and others have renamed these 'code' and 'message'. The code is the language as it exists in the synchronic, the message as it exists in the diachronic. Code underlies message in that message relies on it for communication to be possible at all. But equally, message underlies code in that the code is constituted by the messages which make up actual communication. In short, no communication can occur without an already existing systematized, collectively understandable code, but also the sending of messages by individuals will in the long run modify and restructure the code.

The reason I have mentioned Saussure and Jakobson is that Lévi-Strauss has been strongly influenced by them. Their analysis of language has provided Lévi-Strauss with a model for the study of culture. That is to say, Lévi-Strauss has studied anthropological phenomena such as kinship, totemism, myth as if they were languages.[4] He has examined some of the constituents of cultural behaviour, such as ceremonies, rites, marriage laws, methods of cooking.

Lévi-Strauss, like Marx, believes that much of what is generally considered arbitrary and accidental is in fact determined, and that seemingly gratuitous customs and beliefs are but surface manifestations of a deeper order. He studies the elements of cultural behaviour not as discrete entities, but in terms of the contrastive relationships they have with each other. In his view the structures of cultural behaviour are analogous to the structure of language. Each system, that is, kinship, food, marriage, ritual, cooking, political ideology, etc., constitutes a partial expression of the total culture, conceived ultimately as a single, gigantic language.

One of Lévi-Strauss' main theses is that human beings need to form relations with nature and to mark themselves off from it. Nature is taken by Lévi-Strauss to be that which is common to all human beings and part of their hereditary endowment. Culture is all that is not common, all that has to be learnt. The cultural is, in other words, the contingent and the arbitrary, the natural is the necessary and the absolute. Food is particularly important since it is a direct manifestation of the interpenetration of nature (the raw) and culture (the cooked). Eating is natural in that all people do it, but 'table manners', modes of consumption of food, are in all societies different. Table manners are cultural because they are arbitrary and contingent; salivation is natural because it is universal and instinctual.

This complex relationship between nature and culture is expressed in the form of myth. When understood as part of a corpus, myth is seen to carry messages about the organization of nature and culture, and about their interpenetration and difference. For Lévi-Strauss the study of myth is the study of the structural interrelations of its fundamental units. He calls them mythemes, using this term to underline the parallel with the phoneme of structural linguistics. In his view phenomena such as myth, kinship and totemism are analogous in their structure to language and function as codes. The discourse of myths does possess a principle of reasoning, but it is not of syllogistic logic. Lévi-Strauss argues that the mind splits and opposes, mediates and resolves by use of a binary structural logic.

This notion is analogous to that found by Jakobson in phonetics. Jacobson said that all differences of phonemes (the speech sounds of which a word is composed) in any language can be resolved into simple binary oppositions. Developing this idea further, Lévi-Strauss contends that tendencies to construct binary oppositions are fundamental to thought.

Myth and music, for example, are structurally very similar. In music the diachronic dimension is the melody, the synchronic is the harmony. Myths can be seen as a 'score' in which the 'melody' reads diachronically from left to right, and the harmony reads synchronically up and down.[5] The total myth story is divided into a sequence of episodes. Each episode is a partial metaphoric transformation of every other. One mythemic transformation at the beginning of a myth may 'harmonize' with another at the end and, indeed, only derive its significance from this relation. Mythemes may also harmonize with those in other myths. These 'harmonies' in myths operate on the principle of uniformity or opposition. Myths, in short, are a means of structuring and ordering reality, a means of understanding it. Myths express contradictions and provide ways of settling them; they contain a logic for explaining the world.

Structuralism, then, is not concerned with the 'surface' of social life as consciously experienced by the members of the community. Lévi-Strauss is concerned with how myths **think** in people, without the deeper meanings of the myths being known to them. Myths embody the distinction between *langue* and *parole:* the individual version of each myth, its *parole*, derives from and contributes to the fundamental structure of its *langue.* He is concerned with the *langue* of the myth that lies behind all its *paroles.*

According to the traditional view, the world consists of independently existing objects which can be objectively observed and classified. Structuralism undermines what Lévi-Strauss calls 'sterile empiricism', the notion that the real world consists of a single undeniable reality. In a structure there is a system of relationships governed by general laws which determine the status of every individual item it contains. Structuralism probes like an X-ray beyond apparently independently existing concrete objects, beyond an 'item-centred' world, into a relational one.

Lévi-Strauss' approach is original in at least three ways. Through the study of cultural symbolism he aims to understand a mode of thinking shared by all humans, irrespective of time or place. He is concerned with the abstract relationship between symbols. He does not ascribe a single interpretation to each symbol, but tries to show that symbols are open to a great variety of different and complementary interpretations.

Lévi-Strauss argues against the notion that primitive people are incapable of abstract thought. In his view concrete categories (such as food or animals) can serve as intellectual tools to express abstract notions and relationships, and that untamed thinking tends to order its world in this way. Whereas western societies have developed abstract categories and mathematical operations, other cultures use a logic whose procedures are similar but whose categories are more concrete and hence metaphorical. I will return to this point at the end of the chapter.

Lévi-Strauss believes that there is no way of deciding for each item separately which of its many features would be salient in a given culture. He suggests that if relationships between items are considered, then shared or contrasted features stand out as the basis for symbolic associations. In short, when trying to establish facts which are universally true of the human mind, one should study systems of relationships; not symbols, but symbolic systems.

At first glance structuralism does not seem to have much in common with Althusserian marxism as I have depicted it in the previous chapters. But, as Stuart Hall has correctly pointed out, the manner in which Althusser attempted to rethink structuralism on marxist foundations owed much more to Lévi-Strauss (and through him, inevitably, to Durkheim) than he or his followers have been willing to acknowledge.[6] Consider the similarities: Althusser, like Lévi-Strauss, has an anti-empiricist conception of reality. Both Althusser and Lévi-Strauss study the relationship between structural elements, not the acts of individuals. They believe that structures are based on a limited number of elements, which may be combined in a finite number of ways to produce different but related social realities. Finally, they both consider the criterion of validity of their theory to be intelligibility rather than verification or falsification.[7] Let us now turn from anthropology and the study of myth to a deeper consideration of literature.

Structures of Literature

The Russian formalist movement flowered in the USSR before and during the 1920s. The formalists, a group of like-minded scholars, included Viktor Shklovsky, V. Propp, Boris Eichenbaum, Jurij Tynyanov, Roman Jakobson and others. Their main concern was the study of the techniques by which literary language works. They were not interested in biographical, psychological, sociological or historical dimensions. What was important was not the author but the structure of the work, its *formal* properties, how it was constructed.[8]

For the formalists the individual work of art stands out as a sort of *parole* in relation to its parent *langue*. They showed that even though many stories seem different on the surface, a structural analysis reveals that they spring from a common 'grammar'. In other words, the formalists approached a given text in the same way that Saussure approached a unit of language. Just as the function and meaning of the latter is determined not by its origin but by its relationship to other such units of meaning within the system of relationships comprised by *la langue*, so the function and meaning of a text derives from its relationship to other texts within a given literary system. Literature is a kind of *langue*, an autonomous, internally coherent, self-limiting, self-regulating, self-justifying structure.

Most traditional texts convey the illusion that they are literal transcriptions of reality. Against this view formalists like Viktor Shklovsky argued that literature was not a reflection of reality but an organized signification of it. Far from reflecting reality, literary texts tend to 'make it strange', to dislocate our habitual perceptions of the real world so as to make it the object of a renewed attentiveness. To put this in another way: whilst traditional modes of writing encourage the reader to read *through* the formal artistic devices without noticing them, the formalists preferred those forms of writing which made the reader aware of the devices being used. They favoured contemporary avant-garde literary practice which 'defamiliarizes' conventions, reveals them as conventions and in so doing shows how they condition our perceptions of reality, by refusing to conform to them.[9] Their studies, therefore, set out to reveal the formal mechanisms whereby the effect of defamiliarization was produced. This raises for me the important question: is this process idealist and apolitical or does it really have material effects? The formalists regarded defamiliarization as a purely aesthetic matter. In contrast, another group, the futurists, saw the disruption of habitualized ways of seeing as a means for promoting political awareness. Let us now turn to the question of whether political awareness can be developed in schools and colleges through the use of new approaches in the teaching of literature.

New Approaches

Literature has an importance in England that perhaps philosophy occupies on the Continent, and there are many conflicting views on the teaching of the subject. The typical 'liberal' view is that literature is valuable because it gives an understanding of our lives and that of others, it helps us develop an empathy with ways of life in other places and times. Against this view marxists point out that the literature studied has been selected by dominant groups in their interest. Now, though many teachers campaign against this injustice and argue for a wider canon (a syllabus that includes, for example, working-class novels), it seems to me that very little is said about the approaches that could be used.

I want to argue that views about literature involve assumptions about language and about meaning, and these in turn involve presuppositions about human society. For example, in the English departments of most schools and colleges the assumptions of realism are currently perpetuated. By realism is meant the theory that literature reflects the reality of experience as it is perceived by an exceptionally gifted individual, who expresses it in a way which enables other people to recognize it as true.[10] Realism refers to those fictional forms which create the illusion while we read that what is narrated is really happening. Literature is taken to be a reflection of life. Within this theory the text is seen as possessing a single, determinate meaning, and the authority for this meaning is the author.

Now, post-Saussurean work on language has challenged the whole concept of realism. Meaning cannot inhere timelessly within the words on the page. It is language which provides the possibility of meaning, and language is not static, but perpetually in process. Structuralism, or more precisely, post-Saussurean theory, starts from an analysis of language, proposing that language is not transparent, not merely the medium in which autonomous individuals transmit messages to each other about an independently constituted world of things. Language offers the possibility of constructing a world of individuals and things, and of differentiating between them.

What are the key features of the new approaches as they are being applied in the study of literature? From a structuralist perspective, as I have already briefly alluded, art is seen as production. There is an attempt to go beyond traditional theories of art (as representation, as a transparent reflection of reality) and to introduce instead the notion of art as 'work', art as a 'practice', a particular transformation of reality. The emphasis is not on the private experience of the individual author but on the text as a constructed artifact, the materials and their arrangement in the work. The notion of the author as a mysterious genius has disappeared and has been replaced by a worker transforming a given raw material through the methodical employment of a determinate means of production.[11]

This approach draws on an alternative theory of aesthetics, rooted in modernism and the avant-garde, and takes as its model

Brecht's idea of an 'epic theatre'. Brecht wrote a new kind of text which foregrounded contradiction rather than effaced it. He distanced the audience by preventing audience identification with character. Plot continuity and easy resolutions were rejected. The purpose of this sort of writing is to jar the audience into the recognition that reality is alterable. One could call such works interrogative texts.

It has been suggested that there are three kinds of texts: declarative, imperative, and interrogative.[12] Declarative texts include realist works. The imperative text, which gives orders to its readers, is what is commonly thought of as propaganda. The interrogative text tends to undermine illusionism and draws attention to its own textuality. It disrupts the unity of the reader by discouraging identification with a unified subject. It refuses a single point of view. These three categories are in no sense self-contained and mutually exclusive, nor are their characteristics timelessly sealed within specific texts. Of course a different way of reading can transfer a text from one category to another.

Some marxists argue that, as the function of literature is ideological, to create hegemonic control, the task of radical teachers is to make their students critical of the dominant assumptions and structures through the deconstruction of bourgeois literature. It is argued that if the text is a construct it is available for 'deconstruction' — the analysis of the process and conditions of its construction out of the available discourses. The object of deconstructing the text is to examine the process of its production — not the private experience of the individual author, but the mode of production, the materials and their arrangement in the work. The aim is to locate the contradictions within the text, the points at which it transgresses the limits within which it is constructed.

Roland Barthes

A significant contribution to modern structuralism has been made by Roland Barthes. He has argued that all aspects of bourgeois life silently acquire the same air of naturalness, of rightness, of universality and inevitability. How does this happen? He contends that bourgeois writing is not innocent. It does not simply reflect reality, in fact it *shapes* reality in its own image, acting as the institutionalized transmitter of the bourgeois way of life and its values. To respond to such writing is to accede to those values, to confirm and to reinforce the nature of that way of life.[13]

Barthes has also written about contemporary 'myth' — the complex system of images and beliefs which a society constructs in order to sustain and authenticate its sense of its own being. [14] That is to say, myths (in Barthes' work) are forms of representation in which ideological meanings come to seem natural; they eternalize the present state of the world in the interests of the bourgeois class. He argues that there is a necessity for a dominant order to present itself as a natural order. Myth is a particular use of language to naturalize, dehistoricize a humanly-created reality. Barthes wants to show that what appears to be unchangeable is humanly created and can be recreated.

Barthes has made many criticisms of traditional literary studies. He argues that in the past literary criticism was predominantly ahistorical, working, as it did, on the assumption that the moral and formal values of the texts it studied were timeless. He also feels that academic criticism is psychologically naive and deterministic. It operates with a model of the human personality made obsolete by the discoveries of psychoanalysis. In fact, he actually tries to show that it is possible to psychoanalyze a text, uncover its obsessions, its evasions, and so forth. Another objection to the academic critics was that when they looked at texts they usually saw only one, literal meaning and discouraged the search for alternative meanings. Barthes contends that conventional criticism aims at a closure of troubling plurality; it aims at finding a source (the author) and an ending, a closure. [15]

For Barthes the relationship between writer and reader is a complex social, political, and even economic affair. The process involves codes which modify, determine, and generate meaning. His work undermines the idea that a text has a unitary meaning injected into it by a unitary author. This is part of a larger attack on the illusions of individualism which ultimately has a political and economic origin. He remarks that whilst most post-Renaissance authors tend to think of their writing as an expression of their individuality, medieval authors did not. There was no real concept of personal authorship in the Middle Ages because works were then seen as part of a collective enterprise. In short, Barthes aims to undermine the perpetuation of a particular vision of reality through the institutionalizing of a particular series of 'classic' texts and of appropriate 'interpretations' of them. Barthes believes that the educational system, which processes all members of society, acts as a potent 'normalizing' force.

Barthes' achievement was that he shifted the critics' responsibility in respect of meaning by attending not to the product but to the system whereby it is produced, not to significance but to the process of signification. In his view traditional critics were able to give the illusion that their values were universal ones beyond challenge, not the values of a given class in a given society at a given moment of its history. This mystification endowed historical or cultural phenomena with all the appearance of natural ones.

The answer to mystification was demystification through a new form of writing. Barthes made a qualitative distinction between two sorts of writers. The lesser sort is the *écrivant* for whom language is the means to some extra-linguistic end. He is a transitive writer in that he has a direct object. He intends that whatever he writes should carry one meaning only, the meaning he himself wants to transmit to his readers.

The other sort of writer writes intransitively in so far as he devotes his attention to the means, which is language, instead of the end. The *écrivain* is a materialist, working with the materiality of language, but he is also a worker. A finished work is not a product of magic and inspiration, but of intellectual labour. Whilst the *écrivain* produces a Text, the *écrivant* produces a Work. Texts are *scriptible* because the reader as it were rewrites them as he reads. Works, on the other hand, are *lisible* or readable; we do not rewrite them but simply read them from start to finish. We proceed horizontally through a Work, but vertically, if that is possible, through a Text. In short, the readable (*lisible*) text is merchandise to be consumed; such a text moves inevitably and irreversibly to an end, to the conclusion of an ordered series of events, to the disclosure of what has been concealed. The writable (*scriptible*) text requires the production of meanings, the active participation of the reader.

Barthes has said that the goal of literary work is to make the reader no longer a consumer, but a producer of the text. Barthes owes to Brecht the distinction between the passive consumer of the readable (*lisible*) realist text and the active producer of meaning who accepts the challenge of the writable (*scriptible*) text. Finally, there are two modes of response: *plaisir* is the mode of response to the *lisible*; *jouissance* is appropriate to writing that is *scriptible*. *Plaisir* is merely pleasurable, but *jouissance* is much deeper and can be disconcerting: it can rock the reader's psychological, cultural and historical foundations.[16]

In the new approaches to literature which I am trying to describe there is no absolute distinction between 'form' and 'content' of a work of art. It is held that the ways in which things are said (the narrative structures employed) impose limitations on what can be said. The notion that a detachable content can be inserted into a more or less neutral form (the assumption that seems to underpin the aesthetic of realism) is illusory.

What is important is not just what a text says but what it does. The simple notion of reading as a revelation of a fixed number of concealed meanings is discarded in favour of the idea of a text having a potentially infinite range of meanings. This approach stresses the position of the speaking subject in discourse and is concerned with the process of meaning-construction rather than with the final product.

To reiterate some of the main points: it is increasingly accepted that there is no area of production without ideological influences. Secondly, there is a realization that literature can no longer be seen as 'free-floating', but must be sited in history. Thirdly, the emphasis is on the active reader, the view that the reader produces the text. Finally, it is being recognized that literature cannot be studied in isolation, it is a part of cultural studies.

Semiology and Youth Culture

Structuralism is a method of analysis linking the fields of linguistics, anthropology and semiology. But what is semiology? Semiology is the study of signs, systems of signs.[17] It declares that every message is made of signs, that every social practice has a meaning. Meanings are construed not by their apparent content, but by their relations within a general system of signification. For semiologists any aspect of human activity carries the potential for serving as, or becoming, a sign. Nothing in the human world is merely utilitarian. The world is a text.

In this section I want to bring together some of the ideas of Lévi-Strauss and Barthes and show their relevance for teachers' understanding of pupils. I will give a brief description of how structuralism can provide a way of analyzing youth culture. The work of Lévi-Strauss, which stresses the fact that any culture may be looked upon as an ensemble of symbolic systems, has been found useful in the study of youth subcultures. Barthes' application of a method rooted in linguistics to other systems, such as fashion, film, food, etc., has also opened up exciting possibilities for cultural studies.

It is sometimes assumed that schools are very powerful ideological institutions. Schools, it is said, have monopoly ownership of the children's time, and so oppositional values rarely emerge. But some research suggest that working-class youngsters do not accept the bourgeois values fostered by schools. Many pupils are involved in various types of resistance against the (school) system. Some of them identify with youth subcultures more than they do with the culture of the school; they tend either to have contradictory attitudes or to reject school altogether.

It is essential that teachers, social workers and others dealing with young people understand contemporary youth cults: subcultures such as teddy boys, mods, rockers, skinheads and punks. I think it is important to study youth groups as they are manifestations of popular culture opposed to 'official' culture. The tension between dominant and subordinate groups can be found reflected in subculture. Moreover, I believe that popular culture is probably having more influence on young people now than the school system, and that its importance is growing.

In the past many writers tended to attribute an inordinate significance to the conflict between young and old, child and parent. The persistence of *class* as a meaningful category within youth culture was not generally acknowledged until fairly recently. According to Dick Hebdige, the skinheads constituted an identifiable subculture by the late sixties.[18] Aggressively proletarian, puritanical and chauvinist, the skinheads dressed down in sharp contrast to their mod antecedents in a uniform which has been described as a kind of caricature of the model worker. These cultures have been interpreted as being concerned about the process of social mobility. Whereas the mods explored the upward mobile option, the skinheads explored the working-class one. Punks, who claimed to speak for white 'lumpen' youth, openly identified with Black British and West Indian culture, but this served to antagonize the teddy boy revivalists.

The idea of subcultural style as a coded response to changes affecting the entire community has transformed the study of youth culture. According to this view, each subculture represents a distinctive 'moment', a particular response to a particular set of circumstances. The skinheads undoubtedly reasserted the values of the traditional working-class community, but they did so at a time when such an affirmation was considered inappropriate, in the face of the widespread renunciation of these values in the parent culture. Consider another example, the punks. This subculture was symptomatic of the whole cluster of contemporary problems. The punks were not only directly responding to increasing joblessness, they were dramatizing Britain's crisis. Subcultures, then, not only breach our expectancies, they are challenges to accepted norms and conventions. But how are subcultural styles constructed?

The Fabrication of Youth Subcultures

Lévi-Strauss' structuralist anthropology approaches a myth, a work of literature, or a social system with an initial act of isolation. Such questions as the intentions of a creative subject, the functional origins of a system, the effects of external factors on the object, or of the object on its environment are set aside as irrelevant. The isolated object is then analyzed in terms of a 'combinatory' system, that is, a system of relations between elements, in which it is the relations rather than the elements that are significant.

One of Lévi-Strauss' concepts, that of *bricolage*, has been used to explain how subcultural styles are constructed. The *bricoleur* is a sort of handyman who will use whatever comes to hand to do a job by inspired 'ad-hocism' rather than with purpose-made parts. Primitive thought uses pre-existing objects to serve new intellectual purposes. This use of existing elements in a new way transforms the elements of thought into *signs*.

It is in *The Savage Mind* that Lévi-Strauss shows how the magical modes utilized by primitive peoples (superstition, sorcery, myth) can be seen as implicitly coherent though explicitly bewildering systems of connection between *things* which equip their users to 'think' their own world.[19]

What happens is that basic elements are used in a variety of improvised combinations to generate new meanings within them. The structures which are formed by these elements are improvised or made up as *ad hoc* responses to an environment. They serve to establish homologies and analogies between the ordering of nature and that of society, and so satisfactorily 'explain' the world. The *bricoleur* relocates a significant object in a different position within a discourse, using the same overall repertoire of signs, or places the object within a different total ensemble, which constitutes a new discourse and conveys a different message.

The visual ensembles of youth subcultures are fabricated in a similar way. Subcultures reposition and recontextualize commodities by subverting their conventional uses and inventing new ones. That is to say, the subcultural stylist originates new and oppositional readings.

The radical practices of Dada and surrealism are also helpful in understanding youth styles. The surrealists wanted to subvert common sense, to celebrate the abnormal and the forbidden. The subcultural *bricoleur*, like the 'author' of a surrealist collage, typically juxtaposes two apparently incompatible realities. There is another similarity: both surrealists and punks have a tendency towards wilful desecration and the voluntary assumption of outcast status. Punk subculture signified chaos, but the chaos cohered as a meaningful whole.

It has been pointed out by Paul Willis and others that the internal structure of any particular subculture is characterized by an extreme orderliness.[20] Each part is organically related to other parts, and it is through the fit between them that the subcultural member makes sense of the world. For example, the skinheads' boots, braces and cropped hair were considered appropriate because they communicated the desired qualities: hardness, masculinity and working-classness.[21] In this way, the symbolic objects — dress, appearance, language, ritual occasions, styles of interaction, music — were made to form a unity with the group's relations, situation, experience.

Thus the punks wore clothes which were the sartorial equivalent of swear-words, torn clothes in cheap, trashy fabrics; they dyed their hair and wore the paraphernalia of bondage: belts, straps and chains. In this way they eloquently condemned an oppressive and exploitative society. Punks self-consciously mirrored the inequality and alienation of contemporary Britain. It was through these adapted forms that certain sections of predominantly working-class youth were able to restate their opposition to dominant values and institutions.

Working-Class Pupils: From Opposition to Defusion

The use of semiology is becoming increasingly popular in cultural studies. It is better than traditional content analysis because it is not concerned merely with the numerative appearance of content, but with what 'contents' signify. What is important is not quantification but understanding messages as structured wholes. An interesting example of the semiological approach is Angela McRobbie's analysis of the schoolgirl magazine *Jackie*.[22] She has drawn out five different subcodes of femininity which relate to beauty, fashion, pop music, personal/domestic life and romance. She argues that notions of femininity and romance are not arbitrary beliefs imposed on working-class girls by ideological apparatuses. They provide resources for negotiating the demands of boys. Femininity plays a central role in the anti-school activities of girls:

> In an institution which holds qualification-orientated activities in the highest esteem, which treats pupils as children and which is dominated by male pupils and teachers, femininity draws together strands of working-class female resistance. By emphasizing femininity and romance, working-class girls define themselves as adult beings ... in contrast to the school definition of them as unsexed children who should be immediately concerned with their academic work. Ironically, the consequences of these solutions to immediate problems are to guide girls to the sphere of domestic labour, waged labour and dependence on the male wage.[23]

It is important to note that McRobbie examines the magazine not just as a social product but also as an active agent in the production of new meanings. She stresses the point that ideological 'work' carried out by these texts is not merely the reproduction of class/gender definitions and relations but their *reconstruction*.

Though subcultures represent challenges to a symbolic order, they are nearly always incorporated. How does this happen? The media, having gradually colonized the cultural and ideological sphere, now play a crucial role in defining our experience for us. They provide us with the most available categories for classifying the social world. It is primarily through the media that experience is organized and interpreted. Press, television, film not only provide groups with images of other groups, they also relay back to working-class people a 'picture' of their own lives. In the media subcultural style provokes a double response; it is alternately celebrated (in the fashion page) and ridiculed or reviled.

There is a simultaneous diffusion and defusion of the youth style, a continual process of recuperation which takes two forms: the commercial and the ideological. In the commodity form there is a conversion of subcultural signs (dress, music, etc.) into mass-produced objects. Each new subculture establishes new trends, generates new looks and sounds which feed back into the appropriate industries. In the ideological form the 'labelling' and redefinition of deviant behaviour by dominant groups — the police, the media, the judiciary — take place.[24] Roland Barthes has written that the petit-bourgeois is a person unable to imagine the Other. The Other is a scandal which threatens his existence. Two basic strategies have been evolved for dealing with this threat. First, the Other can be trivialized, naturalized, domesticated. In short, the difference is simply denied, otherness is reduced to sameness. Alternatively, the Other can be transformed into meaningless exotica.[25] In these ways, the cycle leading from opposition to defusion, from resistance to incorporation, encloses each successive youth subculture.

In short, it is important for teachers to realize that subcultures are forms of resistance in which experienced contradictions and objections to the ruling ideology are obliquely represented in style. Though youth cultural styles are forms of resistance, they are gradually manipulated and recuperated.[26] Symbolic assaults leave real institutions intact.

Chapter 5

The Undermining of Structuralism

In this chapter we move on from structuralism to an exposition of post-structuralism. I will begin with some criticisms that have been made of Saussure's work. These criticisms helped to undermine structuralism and pave the way for new practices. I will focus on the work of the innovative French thinker Jacques Derrida, give an explanation of his notion of deconstruction and relate it to education. The chapter concludes with a discussion of the main characteristics of post-structuralism.

Criticism of Saussure

It has been suggested by the Italian marxist Sebastiano Timpanaro that the historical genesis of structuralism was within the movement of anti-materialist reaction, which had its beginning in the late nineteenth century.[1] The distinctions made by Saussure carry the mark of the cultural climate in which they arose. Saussure's theory is based on an antinomic framework (*langue — parole*, synchrony — diachrony), and he insisted on the need to keep these polar terms absolutely distinct, free from all contaminating influences. The conception of *langue* as a system could not be blurred by a consideration of phenomena dealing with individuals (*parole*). *Langue*, the system of abstract concepts, was stressed at the cost of the changing empirical manifestations. *Parole*, primarily a material manifestation of *langue*, was regarded as irrelevant to the study of language as a system of signs.

Saussure also contended that diachrony was not amenable to rigorous scientific study in that it is the realm of particular and fortuitous phenomena. It was on the basis of synchrony that the systematic nature of language revealed itself. In short, he held a dualistic conception: the pole *parole*-diachrony belongs to the world of becoming, the accidental and the atomistic which is not amenable to science; the pole *langue*-synchrony belongs to the realm of being and science.

Whilst it is true that Saussure foresaw a future science of signs, semiology, of which linguistics represents one part, he always emphasized the *differences* between language and the other human institutions and activities. It is not generally realized that Saussure was not sympathetic to the idea of using the conventional and systematic character of language as a model which can be freely applied to all the other sciences. In Saussure the emphasis is not on the analogy between language and the other institutions, but on the singularity of the former.[2]

Moreover, Saussure did not want to reduce all reality to language, or to a 'system' in a formalistic sense. Nevertheless it must be conceded that in Saussure there is a tendency to detach signs from any relationship with extra-linguistic reality and to define them only in relation to other signs.

One of the main weaknesses of Saussure's theory of language is its inability to account for the processes whereby the system of rules comprising *langue* is subject to change through time. No account is offered of the means whereby *langue* moves from one synchronic state to another. *Langue* was originally conceived as merely a systematization of the rules which make individual speech acts possible. But the structure must, in some way, be capable of transformational procedures whereby new material is constantly processed. And so a tendency has developed to see *langue* not as a concept, but as a real entity with a life and will of its own, an entity which oversees and regulates its own processes. As Tony Bennett has commented:

> As a body of rules pre-existing the individual, *la langue* is conceived of as a totally unitary system ... it gives rise merely to the concept of the ideal-typical speaker and has no room for the concept of different class-based linguistic practices; that is of different communities of speakers who bring different sets of rules into play in their uses of language. Small wonder that change could not be accounted for. For the very motor of change — conflict and difference — had been exiled from the heartland of language.[3]

To recapitulate the main points: in Saussure's theory of language no account is given of how *langue* changes from one synchronic state to another. Secondly, *langue* is often reified; that is to say, it is seen as a real entity with a life and will of its own rather than as a concept. Thirdly, there is no way in which the structure of *langue* can be explained, within Saussure's theory, with reference to determinations which lie outside it. Fourthly, Saussure assumes a pre-given user of language, but the question of the constitution of the subject is never asked. Fifthly, the theory has no room for different class-based practices; that is to say, language as an arena of class-struggle is not considered.[4]

Derrida's Critique

Jacques Derrida has made some cogent criticisms of Saussure (and hence structuralism) and all rationalist theories of language. He is a post-structuralist in the sense that he has developed a critique of the Saussurean concept of the sign on which structuralism rested.[5]

It may be remembered that in Saussure's theory signs are representational, since they have fixed meanings prior to their articulation in any particular speech act. Their meanings are fixed within the language system itself through the arbitrary linking of signifiers (sound images) to signified (concepts). The meaning of the individual sign lies in its difference from all other signs in the language chain. Saussure's theory of language is based implicitly on a rationalist theory of meaning and consciousness, since it rests on a notion of signs as representing ideas which precede any actual utterance and are, consequently, timeless and context-free. It is this aspect of Saussure's theory with its implicit reliance on a notion of unified, fixed, rational consciousness which has been subject to much criticism.

Now, what Derrida has done is this: he has replaced the *a priori* fixed signifieds of Saussure's theory by a concept of *différance*, a term whose sense remains suspended between the two French verbs 'to differ' and 'to defer'. By the use of the concept he draws attention to the differing and deferring of meaning. For Derrida (unlike Saussure) meaning is no longer a function of the difference between fixed signifieds. It is never fixed outside any textual location or spoken utterance and is always in relation to other textual locations in which the signifier has appeared on other occasions. Every articulation of a signifier bears with it the *trace* of its previous articulations. There is no fixed transcendental signified, since the meaning of concepts is constantly referred, via the network of traces, to their articulations in other discourses. Fixed meaning is constantly *deferred*.[6]

In rationalist discourse the fixed concepts which precede any actual speech act have to be articulated via the conscious intention of the individual speaking subject and the speech community at large. Derrida opens the way for a reconceptualization of the speaking subject, not as the intending originator of speech acts, but as an effect of the structure of language. This decentring of the subject, which challenges the primacy of rationalist consciousness, is also a feature of Lacan's work in psychoanalysis. Like Lacan, whose theory will be examined in the next chapter, Derrida is highly critical of those who stress the unity and continuity of the individual subject.

Deconstruction and Education

Whilst I am discussing Derrida's criticism of Saussure, I think it would be useful to briefly mention some of the ideas of this increasingly influential philosopher-critic. Often one hears, for example, the term 'deconstruction'. This term is applied by Derrida to refer to a new theory of 'reading'.[7] Deconstruction describes the ways in which lines of arguments in the texts and their premises are put into question by using the system of concepts within which a text works to challenge the consistency of that system. The practice of deconstruction involves reading texts to uncover their latent metaphysical structure and to show their presuppositions about the nature of reality.

This critical method is based on the neo-Heideggerian claim that most of western thought is a kind of internal debate using certain fixed conceptual oppositions. Derrida suggests that the attempt throughout history to think about the relations of language, truth and reality is continually biased by the misguided oppositions between writing and speech, signifier and signified, the metaphorical and the literal, presence and absence, sense and intellect, nature and culture, male and female. For Derrida dichotomies such as matter and spirit, subject and object, body and soul, text and meaning, interior and exterior, appearance and essence are set up not rationally, but with an implicit preference for one side or the other. He argues that most texts are structured in terms of oppositions and that one of the two terms occupies the more important position and dominates the other.

The deconstructive strategy has two phases. The first he calls 'reversal'. Suppose, for example, we are reading a text promoting idealism, working with a loaded opposition between the ideal and the material. The first move is to reverse this hierarchy, to argue for the priority of the material. Derrida warns that one must give serious consideration to the first opposition and not pass too quickly to transcend it. He also realizes that merely to reverse someone's terms is to continue to work within the same framework, and so a second stage is necessary.

The aim of the second stage is to prevent the old opposition from re-establishing itself. A radical reorganization and redefinition of the conceptual field is required. This is brought about by the introduction of a new term. Whilst the first stage brings about an engagement with the present field, the second stage aims at transforming it so that it cannot reform itself into the old pattern.

It must be admitted that deconstruction is a highly formal method of criticism. At the moment it concentrates largely on what people have written in books. But I think that Derrida's work could still be used in a practical way in educational institutions. I want to suggest that the strategy of deconstruction could be taught in schools as a sort of internal subversion. I realize, of course, that there is always the danger of recuperation. Indeed, Derrida himself has stated that the Anglo-American appropriation of his ideas, at Yale and elsewhere, is an institutional closure of his work on behalf of the dominant ideology. But there is no theory that belongs only to one side; in the context of class struggle developments in theory should, if possible, be utilized by the Left, or they will be used against it.

I believe that it should be possible to work out methods which show to pupils the ways in which oppositions are so loaded as to give one side a privilege. It would help to illuminate the structures of presupposition in apparently 'innocent' textbooks, to demonstrate the hidden use of power in discourse. In short, deconstruction, if pushed to the Left, could be used to disrupt coercive conventions and to challenge the structures of power that depend on those conventions.

There is insufficient space to deal with Derrida's work fully, but I would like to mention another of his concepts that may be useful for teachers to consider: the idea of *supplément*. Derrida argues that when Rousseau writes that education supplements nature, this produces a complicated concept of nature, for it is both something complete in itself, to which education is an addition, and something incomplete, or insufficient, which must be supplemented by education. In the latter case education is needed in order to allow someone's true nature to emerge as what it is. The logic of supplementarity thus makes nature the prior term, a plenitude which was there at the start, but reveals an inherent lack or absence within it and makes education something external and extra, but also an essential condition of that which it supplements.[8] According to Derrida, it thus becomes possible to show that what were conceived as the distinguishing characteristics of the marginal are in fact the defining qualities of the central object of consideration. The marginal in its very marginality turns out to characterize the central object of discussion.

Derrida and Post-Structuralism

After structuralism, post-structuralism. How can this new movement be characterized? Many post-structuralists counter the prevailing notion of a transparent relation between sign and referent, signification and reality. Their central concern is with the implications of form and with what has come to be called the productivity of language. This approach sees language as an active, transitive force which shapes and positions the 'subject' (as speaker, writer, reader) while always itself remaining in process, capable of infinite adaptation.

Althusser's model of the social formation, which specified the relative autonomy of the ideological level, created the space within marxism for serious consideration of the importance of signifying practices.[9] But with the post-structuralists the emphasis on signifying practice (an activity which involves representation by signs and/or symbols) is accompanied by a polemical insistence that art represents the triumph of process over fixity, the signifier over the signified, disruption over unity. The values of fissure and contradiction replace the preoccupation with wholeness and totality which characterized (Lukácsian) marxism.

Saussure's ideas about language have been challenged not only by Derrida but also by other post-structuralists such as Jacques Lacan. They shatter the unity of the signifier and the signified. The materiality of the signifier is stressed and given privilege. Many post-structuralists devalue any closed system and valorize the potential proliferation of meanings. Derrida, in particular, takes the autonomy of language to the extreme; he insists on the total autonomy of texts — which may refer to one another, but not to things outside themselves.

Let me try and make this clearer. In structuralism the emphasis was on the unity of the signifier and the signified which constituted the sign. There was a break with the referent, the world of practical relations. But now the post-structuralists have gone even further. They give priority to the signifier to the extent that the signified disappears. In their view the character of writing generates a permanent gap between any text and any unitary meaning. As Derrida sees it, a text can have no ultimate, final meaning; it is in the nature of writing and of language *not* to be confined to specific structures of meaning. It is argued that this view of writing and of language frees the sign from its subservience to that 'reality' which it was supposed to serve. Seen thus, writing emerges as its own thing, not the creature of some superior reality. Writing does not 'reproduce' a reality beyond itself, nor does it 'reduce' that reality.

In other words, post-structuralists like Derrida and Lacan are saying that the signifier is what we can be sure of, it is material, but the signified is an open question. The same signifier will have different signifieds for the same person at different times. Moreover, the same signifier is sure to have different signifieds for two different people because of the dissimilarity of individual experience. There is, then, no unequivocal interpretation of signs, only the plurality of meaning.

Literary works for the post-structuralists are ultimately about language; their form is their content.[10] Signifiers seem to be prised utterly free of signifieds. In Derrida's theory there is the alarming prospect of a world in which there are no meanings, no transcendent signified.[11] Post-structuralists argue that all literary works are ultimately about themselves, self-reflexive. There seems to be no concrete reality beyond itself to which the work refers: the subject of criticism is not 'the world' but discourse; criticism is discourse about discourse. 'Literature is simply a language, a system of signs. Its being is not in its message, but in this "system". Similarly, it is not for criticism to reconstitute the message of a work, but only its system.'[12]

In conclusion: what do post-structuralists like Derrida, Lacan and Foucault have in common? Post-structuralism has questioned the status of science itself, and the possibility of any language to be objective. The shift of emphasis from the signified to the signifier results in *a refusal to fix meaning*. Secondly, post-structuralism involves *a critique of metaphysics*, of the concepts of causality, of identity, of truth and of the human subject. Thirdly, it acknowledges and *incorporates psychoanalytic modes of thought*.

Derrida, Lacan and Foucault in their different ways have all produced *a critique of the classical conception of the unitary subject*.[13] In humanist philosophies the subject is a unity as consciousness and agent, it is capable of knowing itself (through reflection on that unity) and of being the source of its actions. It is this centredness in consciousness that post-structuralism challenges. Having briefly looked at Derrida, I turn now to a detailed consideration of the psychoanalytic theory of Jacques Lacan.

Chapter 6

The Structuring of Subjectivity

Social Reproduction and Schooling

Before I discuss Lacan's theory about the acquisition and structuring of subjectivity I would like to place his thesis within a social and educational context. In traditional sociology of education, though reference is made to social reproduction, little attention is given to the formation of individual identity. Social reproduction refers to all the various relations and institutions that serve to reproduce society without any fundamental change. In advanced capitalist countries social reproduction occurs in many ways, some of the most important being the social division of labour (the way in which work is organized in society as a whole), the technical division of labour (the manner in which work is organized in the capitalist firm), the state, the family and schooling.

A tacit function of schooling is the teaching of different dispositions and values to different school populations. Indeed, Bowles and Gintis have argued that the most economically important function of school is the selection and generation of personality attributes.[1] Their work emphasizes the importance of schooling in forming the different personality types which correspond to the requirements of the economic system. Schools allocate people to the positions 're-quired' by the economic sector.

The socialization of future workers begins very early. I read recently of an American study where the researcher investigated the interaction between kindergarten (nursery) children and their teacher.[2] It is reported that the children quickly learned to make the distinction between 'work' and 'play'. Work was defined as including all teacher-directed activities. To work was to do what one was told to do, regardless of the nature of the activity involved. The entire class worked on all tasks simultaneously, and all the children were required to complete the assigned tasks during the designated work period. They had to do the same thing at the same time, and the same product was expected of each child. Diligence, perseverance, obedience and participation were rewarded. The children's teacher stated that, as a preparation for the reality of adult work, they needed practice in following directions, without the right of options. Thus the children of nursery age are socialized to restrain their emotional responses and react with prompt obedience. I think such an example enables us to understand one of the processes by which society reproduces itself, how it perpetuates its conditions of existence.

Two important theorists who have focussed on the formation of social identity are Basil Bernstein and Pierre Bourdieu. They believe that the transmission of specific forms of culture through educational institutions ensures not merely the reproduction of that culture, but also of the class structure it supports and is supported by. They argue that *the structural division and relations between forms of knowledge* is a far more significant aspect of the formation of social identities than the actual selection of knowledge and its hidden message. What is important is the acquisition of the rules and principles which govern the structural hierarchies of culture.

Bernstein and Bourdieu suggest that social identities are formed through a process of internalization of the core classifications — those of age, sex and social class. The structures of age relations, sex relations and class relations are to be found, for example, in the family, the work place and the school. What is central to Bernstein's analysis is whether a school subject has high or low status, whether it is compulsory or optional and what relation it bears to other subjects in terms of the strength or weakness of its boundaries.

Bourdieu asks us to think of cultural capital (language, knowledge, good taste) as we would of economic capital. He argues that the cultural capital stored in schools acts as an effective filtering device in the reproduction of a hierarchical society. Schools take the cultural capital of the middle class as natural and employ it as if all children have had equal access to it. However, by taking all children as equal, while implicitly favouring those who have already acquired the linguistic and social competencies to handle middle-class culture, schools take as natural what is essentially a social gift — cultural capital.

It is often claimed that Basil Bernstein's theory of educational codes and Pierre Bourdieu's work on cultural codes are structuralist.[3] But this term has many meanings, and it should be made clear that their 'structuralism' is not based on an application of lingusitics but of the classifications of Durkheim.

In the work of Bernstein and Bourdieu the actual process of socialization through internalization remains vague. It will have been noticed, too, that though Bowles and Gintis are concerned with the generation of personality attributes, dispositions and values, they have no theory of how individual identity is formed. Indeed in most of the marxist tradition the 'subject' has been treated as an empty space. The development by Jacques Lacan of a psychoanalytic theory of language has filled this space in recent years. In this chapter, therefore, I will give an exposition of Lacan's theory of the constitution of the 'subject' (that is to say, the acquisition and structuring of subjectivity), and then make some criticisms of Lacan and the way Lacanian theory has been propagated and used on some 'Media' and 'Cultural Studies' courses.

Lacan, Language and the Constitution of the Subject

Lacan calls for a return to Freud and to the reinstatement of the central concepts of psychoanalysis. He claims that Freud's work can be divided into three phases. In the early phase Freud's work was dominated by a mechanistic, even biological viewpoint. In the middle phase the unconscious is seen as the site of the true person. In the final phase, however, Freud saw human beings in terms of adaptation and adjustment.

Lacan adores the middle phase during which Freud was concerned with language, the interpretation of dreams, and the psychopathology of everyday life.[4] He regards the other phases as 'heresies'; he is antagonisitc to the first phase for its biologism, and he rejects the final phase because of the way ego-psychologists have used therapy for the 'adjustment' of individuals.

Lacan, then, is an anti-adaptationist psychoanalyst, opposed to ego-psychology. For ego-psychologists the ego is the site of the real person and his dealings with the world, with whom unconscious factors interfere. Lacan, however, believes that the ego is the site of the self-for-others which is an alienated and impoverished self. The true self is the unconscious, operating by and through language, erupting into all our lives in ways which we may never control. The identification of the subject with the conscious is both restrictive and repressive because it makes no allowance for the unconscious. In Lacan's view science is ideological to the extent that it denies the unconscious and reduces wishing to an insignificant place in human behaviour.

In other words, Lacan's point of departure is a critique of those theoretical developments which have taken a biologistic direction (Klein, Horney) or developed in the form of ego-psychology (Erikson). He challenges the principle of a unified, intentional consciousness as the source of meaning, and insists on the primacy, within Freudian psychoanalysis, of the unconscious. For him Freud's essential insight was not that the unconscious exists, but that it has a structure, that this structure affects in innumerable ways what we say and do, and that in thus betraying itself it becomes accessible to analysis. The unconscious reveals itself in dreams, forgettings, misrememberings, jokes and slips of the tongue.[5] Lacan points out that the discovery of the unconscious is itself subject to repression.

Lacan's work demonstrates the ways in which structural linguistics may be used to reorganize the psychoanalytic account of the unconscious. He draws upon the work of Saussure and Jakobson. It may be remembered that Saussure stressed the arbitrary nature of language, that words were signs. A sign consists of a signifier and signified; the sound or printed letter is the signifier, the concept to which it refers is the signified. (The object represented by the sign, the referent, lay outside the linguists' area of concern.) Roman Jakobson extended Saussure's theories and applied them in particular to folk tales and works of literature.[6] Jakobson lay particular stress on metaphor (one thing standing for another) and metonymy (a part standing for the whole).

Lacan, taking the concept of the linguistic sign from Saussure and the use of metaphor and metonymy from Jakobson, pointed out that not only could dreams be analyzed like works of literature, but the unconscious itself was 'structured like a language'. The world did not enter the unconscious directly or in images, but through language, through signifiers, which usually had no more than an arbitrary relation to their referents, to the real objects. To put it simply, language creates the unconscious. The human subject, as it acquires speech, is inserting itself into a pre-existing symbolic order and thereby submitting the libido (*désir*) to the systemic pressures of that order; in adopting language, it allows its free instinctual energies to be operated upon and organized.

The analogue for language acquisition is, for Lacan, contained in Freud's discussion of the *fort/da* game. The game involved an 18-month-old child making objects disappear and reappear to the accompaniment of noises, noises similar to the German words for 'there it goes' (*fort*) and 'here it is' (*da*). Freud provided several interpretations of the game; one was that the game could be seen to represent the achievement of instinctual renunciation, allowing the child to master the anxiety associated with the periodic and inexplicable absences of the mother. The *fort/da* game enabled the child to symbolize a control over the presence and absence of objects — and the mother.

Lacan follows the above interpretation; it is the experience of the absence and presence of the mother which institutes the earliest use of language. The child learns language (or rather, basic linguistic units, perhaps phonemes) as s/he learns the renunciation of instincts; s/he rejects the infinity of desires and accepts the finitude of demands. At the same time, language learning leads to the development of a distinction between self and others. There is a split between discourse which provides a subject-for-others (an ego) and discourse about a 'true' subject, the 'discourse of the unconscious'. In short, the *fort/da* game forms the basis for language usage, the substitution of desire by demand, and the alienation of the self.

The Development of Self

Let us now turn to Lacan's model for the child's discovery of self and of others. His theorization of the acquisition and structuring of subjectivity and language has a psychosexual basis in child development. The young infant is unable to distinguish between things associated with its own body and the external world. In this pre-Oedipal stage it has no sense of its physical separateness from the rest of the world, nor of its physical unity as an organism. The initial conscious recognition by the infant of the distinction between its own body and the outside world comes at about 6 months, with the beginning of the 'mirror' stage.

Self-recognition in the mirror (which precedes language acquisition) occurs in three stages. Firstly, the child confuses the reflection with reality, trying to touch it, looking behind the mirror and, if with an adult, confusing the two images. Secondly, the child realizes that the image in the mirror is not the real thing. Finally, s/he realizes that the image is of her/himself and is different from the images of other people. This 'mirror stage' is the first articulation of the 'I'.

It is language which provides the possibility of subjectivity because it is language which enables the speaker to posit himself or herself as 'I', as the subject of a sentence. It is only with its entry into language that the child becomes a full subject. In order to speak the child is compelled to differentiate 'I' from 'you'. In order to formulate its needs the child learns to identify with the first person singular pronoun, and this constitutes the basis of subjectivity. Subsequently, it learns to recognize itself in a series of subject positions ('boy', 'girl', 'he', 'she', etc.).

Lacan writes that language exists prior to any individual speaking subject, and it is by taking up the position of speaking subject that the human individual acquires gendered, conscious subjectivity. In Lacan's view desire is the structuring principle of the psyche, of language and of subjectivity. It is the manifestation of the *lack* experienced by the individual because he or she is not the source of the laws of human culture and does not control them, but is subjected to them and to the subject positions they make available. The lack of control is manifested in the individual through the gap between need, demand and satisfaction.

This distinction between need, demand and desire is central to Lacan's account. The human individual sets out with certain biological needs. The child's helplessness to attend to his/her own needs results in the detour of need through language into demand, and it is this detour which generates unconscious desire as a fundamental and unfillable 'lack'. Lacan asserts that all speech is demand; it presupposes the Other to whom it is addressed. There is no adequation between the need and the demand that conveys it; indeed, it is the gap between them that constitutes desire.

It should be pointed out that for Lacan desire is not sexual, it is rather the Hegelian notion of recognition by the other.[7] (Lacan was influenced by Hegel's work through Kojeve.) There are two problems: the first is that signs of recognition are always ambiguous; the second is that even if the sign is clear, it is never what you are. *The subject can never fully identify itself with what the other recognizes it to be.*

But why does the subject accept society and its rules? To answer this question we will have to continue the story: after the mirror stage the first form of identification with an object outside the infant is the infant's identification with the mother. Then the infant is faced with a rival, the 'Father', against whom it is powerless.

The Oedipus complex is the term given to the stage when the intervention of the father necessitates the child's abandonment of its exclusive relation with the mother. The father is the possessor of the phallus. Faced with the threat of castration, the infant can only resolve the situation by submitting to the paternal authority at the same time as identifying with that authority.

Lacan gives the Oedipus complex special prominence; for him the father takes a linguistic form, which he calls the Name-of-the-Father. The father is the law-giver; he condemns the individual to non-satisfaction of desire and legislates for society's rules. In the Oedipus situation sexuality is subjected to social rules and restrictions. After a number of stages there is identification of the child with the father. This involves a recognition on the child's part that language is the privileged realm of the father. Language is the gain for the loss of desire and of the mother.

The Possibility of Change

What Lacan did was to take the Freudian concept of the psyche and show that it cannot be assimilated to the philosophical notion of a unitary subject. The ego was all too readily identified as the true centre of the psyche, as a kind of knowing, responsible subject. Lacan showed that, on the contrary, the ego could be seen as a kind of convenient illusion, an 'imaginary' construct, composed of projections and introjections. All three Freudian topographies — the division between conscious and unconscious, between id, ego and superego, and between Eros and Thanatos (the life and death drives) — were not so much expressions of the contrary forces within a unitary psyche as an indication of a deeply riven psyche, a psyche without unity or centre.

Until Lacan, most post-Freudian psychoanalysts tended, especially in America, to stress the ego, the inter-personal relations of the individual. For Lacan the ego is no more than an imaginary precipitate, and so it is absurd for 'ego-psychologists' to dedicate themselves to the task of developing that entity. He is scornfully critical of the ego as a threatened residence of selfhood needing continually to be refortified against hostile incursions from the id and the superego. Traditional psychology has an inveterate tendency to describe the mind as if it were a stable collection of forces or faculties.

In contrast, Lacan's account of the psychical apparatus at work has at its centre the notion not of 'ego' but of 'subject'. The human subject is a linguistic construct alienated at its very source, because not only did the language that made it up come from outside itself and could not, therefore, be an adequate expression of its desire, but language was the bearer of society's prohibitions, of the super-ego, and was therefore a bar to the subject's desire.

Lacan has argued that Freud decentred the human being just as

Copernicus decentred the cosmos. Freud, in challenging the Cartesian basis of liberal humanism, the concept of personality determined by conscious subjectivity, challenged the ideology of liberal humanism itself. Whilst Descartes stressed the notion 'I think, therefore I am', Lacan disconcerts by telling us, 'I think where I am not, therefore I am where I do not think'.[8] Lacan insists that the unconscious is not a repository of biological drives, but, like subjectivity, a construct created in the moment of entry into the symbolic order.

Constructed of elements whose entry into the symbolic order is barred, the unconscious is structured like a language. Lacan argues that entry into the symbolic order liberates the child into the possibility of social relationship; it also reduces its helplessness to the extent that it is now able to articulate its needs in the form of demands. But at the same time a division within the self is constructed. In offering the child the possibility of formulating its desires, the symbolic order also betrays them, since it cannot formulate those elements of desire which remain unconscious. The subject is thus the site of contradiction and is consequently perpetually in the process of construction.

Now, this is in contrast to the ideology of liberal humanism which emphasizes the fixed identity of the individual. This bourgeois ideology assumes a world of non-contradictory and therefore fundamentally unalterable individuals whose unfettered consciousness is the origin of meaning. I would want to argue that it is in the interest of bourgeois ideology to present the individual as a free, unified, autonomous subject.

What Lacan suggests is that the individual is not in reality a harmonious and coherent totality; he emphasizes instead the precariousness of conscious subjectivity. Subjectivity is not a pre-given, fixed human characteristic as rational philosophy presupposes, but is a function of language. As such it is continually 'in process', in the sense that it is reconstituted every time we use language, whether to ourselves or to others. In the fact that the human being is not a unity, not autonomous, but a process, perpetually in construction, perpetually contradictory, lies the possibility of change.

Lacanian Psychoanalysis and Marxism

The Lacanian emphasis on 'the subject in process', on the existence of contradiction and transformation, is one of the main themes of the book *Language and Materialism.*[9] Its authors, Rosalind Coward and John Ellis, argue that marxist thought has not provided an adequate explanation of the individual and assert that it is only psychoanalysis which has gone any way to analyzing the formation of the individual. The key figure in their book is therefore Lacan, who they say has provided a radically different way of situating the problems of language, ideology and the subject.

Though their general theoretical position is based on structuralism, Coward and Ellis are critical of some mechanistic tendencies within it. Like others who have been influenced by Althusser they are antagonistic towards Hegelian and humanist marxism because of its association with idealism. They are also very critical of 'economism'. It is often the case that those theorists who want to focus their attention on ideological practice, semiology, or discourse justify their own stance by attacking economic determinism. It seems to me that this is largely a rhetorical device, as the type of crude economism depicted is now rarely found in marxism.

The positive aim of Coward and Ellis is to link some aspects of structuralist literary theory (Barthes) with the structuralist re-reading of psychoanalysis (Lacan) and an amended Althusserian marxism. Their book is really a popularization of an intellectual synthesis advocated by Julia Kristeva, Philippe Sollers and others associated with the journal *Tel Quel.*

Basically Coward and Ellis make two proposals. First, marxism and (Lacanian) psychoanalysis should be integrated: 'Marxism requires an encounter with psychoanalysis, since it is only the latter which can provide a scientific elaboration of subjective processes and their construction in relation to language.'[10] Secondly, they propose language as a fourth practice (in addition to the economic, political, and the ideological): 'Signifying practice thus provides through psychoanalysis, what the marxist notion of ideological practice elides; it shows the constitution of a necessary positionality, which is the language-using subject.'[11] In their view 'it is the concentration on language — language producing the subject and therefore the unconscious — which points a way to avoiding incorrect appropriations of psychoanalysis to Marxist thought.'[12]

I agree with some of their remarks on structuralism. Individual subjectivity is neglected in structuralism, and I do want to place a greater stress on process. I am sympathetic to their project, their hope that the encounter of psychoanalysis and marxism on the terrain of language should lead to an analysis of the unconscious as a vital element in ideological struggle. But their claim that 'until Marxism can produce a revolutionary subject, revolutionary change will be impossible' is surely going too far?[13] Whilst I agree that the subjective moment is vital for political struggle, I would argue that it should not be over-privileged as it is in many psychoanalytic accounts in which the basis of revolution becomes the individual. I would assert that change of subject is not *necessarily* prior to the change of circumstances. On the contrary, it can be achieved, as Marx pointed out, by means of revolutionary practice: 'the coincidence of the changing of circumstances and of human activity or self-changing can be conceived and rationally understood only as revolutionary practice.'[14]

A feature of the work of Coward and Ellis that I deplore is their unreserved espousal of the theories of Julia Kristeva. They see her work as a real beginning of a materialist theory of language. I am unconvinced about this. In order to explain my position it may be useful to refer, at this point, to her views on avant-garde texts.

The texts of which Kristeva and other structuralists think highly are those of Mallarmé, Lautréamont, Artaud, and Joyce — texts that produce multiple meaning in the process of reading.[15] Coward and Ellis say that these texts are admired because what is revealed in them 'is that part of language which is beyond communication of content; it returns as musicality, rhythm, and productivity ... the constant sliding of signifiers that constitutes *Finnegans Wake* gives a vague indication of this textual practice to which we refer.'[16] In these works the signifier is no longer linked to the signified in a relationship of identity. There is a constant sliding of signifiers which de-establishes positionality — a process similar to the constant sliding of meaning that occurs in dreams.

Kristeva's view, which Coward and Ellis support, is that avant-garde texts produce heterogeneous contradictions which explode the confines of experience. In other words, fixed positions of significations are disrupted to produce a subject in process, a subject crossed by the contradictory processes of society. In my view Kristeva's belief that radical changes in the signifying practices of texts are equivalent to revolutionary practice (since both rely on the destruction of fixed, unified, constant subjectivity) is inadequate.

Screen Theory

Lacan's work has been taken up by theorists in many fields. I want now to look at one appropriation of Lacan's work, namely by writers on film whose views have been called 'screen theory', a theory similar to that expounded by Coward and Ellis, which is often used in Communication and/or Cultural Studies.[17]

Screen theory draws extensively not only on Lacan's psychoanalytical writings, but on Althusser's theory of ideology and Foucault's theories of language and discourse. Writers in the journal *Screen and Screen Education* have constantly emphasized the inadequacy of theories which assumed that 'reality' was transparently reflected in language. Secondly, they reject the notion of the integral Cartesian subject, the authorial 'I', assumed to be both the source and the guarantor of the truth. The Cartesian subject was displaced, but in Lévi-Strauss' myth, in Barthes' codes and Althusser's theories of ideology 'the subject' was left as an empty space.

'Screen theory' fills this gap by drawing on the writings of Lacan and his description of how the unformed infant becomes a 'subject'. As I have already pointed out, this is no longer the unitary individual, the integral and homogeneous 'subject' of Descartes, but a contradictory subject, constantly changing, constituted by unconscious processes. These propositions were reinforced by Althusser's writings on ideology (described in chapter 1) which stress the notion that all ideologies 'work' by and through the constitution of the 'subject'.[18] In short, 'screen theory' breaks with empiricist theories of language, aims to account for how biological individuals become social subjects, and stresses signification as a practice for the production of meaning.

Criticisms of Lacan

What criticisms can be made of Lacan's theory and the way his work is being used in 'screen theory'? Lacan's writing is very difficult to understand because of its unclarity. He rarely uses empirical data and he does not, as Freud did, give us detailed case studies. All his statements are assertions. Lacan always seems to deny the significance of material factors and the somatic. He ignores the natural and physical aspects of human beings, their drives and instincts, the constraints of material existence. With Lacan all aspects of the person and the social relationships become reduced to symbols. For example, the real father of the Freudian Oedipus drama becomes in Lacan the Name-of-the-Father, a mere linguistic symbol.

I would like readers to compare what Saussure says about the signifier-signified relationship with what Lacan says about it. On examining the relevant pages in Saussure's *Course in General Linguis-*

tics one sees that he puts the signified (the concept) over the signifier (the sound image).[19] Not only are they intimately united, each recalling the other, but they are part of a *whole* — this is indicated by an oval shape around the signifier and the signified. Compare this view with Lacan's (mis)-interpretation in *Écrits* where the algorithm S/s is read as: 'the signifier over the signified, "over" corresponding to the bar separating the two stages'. Here the signifier is being given primacy; there is no oval sign indicating the identity of signifier and signified, and the algorithm is in 'two stages'. Lacan indicates that there is no way by which we can 'read off' the meaning automatically; there is no one-to-one correspondence between signifier and signified. There is no immediate transition from signifier to signified. Rather than a unity of signifier and signified we have a constant relay of signifiers, interlinked chains of signifiers rooted in the unconscious. He insists on the term signifier because it is a principle of his theory that meaning cannot be fixed *a priori* in a particular signified. There can be no such thing as denotative meaning. The function of language for Lacan is not to inform but to evoke.[20]

I have stressed the point that in Lacanian theory the only way in which the unconscious can exist, can be known, is through language. Now, to use language as a source of models of the processes of the unconscious is one thing and quite legitimate. All disciplines borrow from others in this manner. It is another matter to conflate the two. The unconscious may be structured like a language, but this is insufficient to support the assumption that the unconscious is a linguistic phenomenon, or that language emanates from the unconscious.

Another criticism of Lacan is that he treats the unconscious as the authentic self and a source of deep wisdom, but it has been argued that there is nothing particularly wise or authentic about the unconscious. It has been suggested by Andrew Collier that Lacan misunderstood Freud on this point and that Lacan's stress on the unconscious as the authentic self is a form of romantic irrationalism. Freud was never hostile to feelings and desires, only to the contradictory properties that prevent their fulfilment; he wanted an increase in our self-awareness and conscious self-direction. The aim of psychoanalysis for Freud was 'to strengthen the ego, to make it more independent of the superego, to widen its field of perception and enlarge its organization, so that it can appropriate fresh portions of the id. Where id was, there ego shall be. It is a work of culture — not unlike the draining of the Zuider Zee.'[21]

A further objection to Lacanian theory is its inadequate

theorization of female sexuality. It could be argued that the eternal privileging of the penis/phallus in the structure of the symbolic order and the unconscious makes Lacanian theory necessarily patriarchal, like that of Lévi-Strauss, on which to some extent it draws.[22]

Moreover, any account of sexed identity which locates the constitution of women so massively in the first few years of life cannot provide a full understanding of the role of women in the social relations of production. As Terry Lovell has pointed out, 'the individual is not constituted as a social subject within a timeless and classless patriarchal order, nor does that individual, already sexed through his/her induction into the patriarchal order of the family, then acquire class identity upon entry to the labour market and economic production. The antagonistic relations between labour and capital are already present within the familial forms of capitalism.'[23]

The Need for a Maxist Theory of the Subjective

Let me now turn to criticisms of 'screen theory'; in some journals the politics of ideological struggle has become exclusively a problem of and around subjectivity in the Lacanian sense — all ideological contestation takes place at the level of the subject. In contrast, historical materialism attempts to relate ideologies to political and economic practices, to their functioning and effectivity in specific social formations.

'Screen theory' privileges one explanatory theory. It is the psychoanalytic process by which the 'subject' is constituted. As Stuart Hall has pointed out:

> The mechanisms which Freud and Lacan identify are, of course, universal. All 'subjects' in all societies at all times are unconsciously constituted in this way. The formation of the subject in this sense is trans-historical and trans-social. It is a theory of the universal 'contradictory' subject — different from the 'subject' of classical philosophy in being intersected by contradiction and unconsciously constituted, but similar to it in the transcendental/universal form in which it is predicated. It is ... impossible to square this universal form of argument with the premises of historical materialism ... which historicizes the different forms of subjectivity and which needs a reference to specific modes of production, to definite societies at historically specific moments and con-

junctures. The two kinds of theory are conceptually incompatible in the form of their argument.[24]

In its present form 'screen theory' refuses to countenance any propositions about discourse or ideology which are not reducible to, and explicable by, the Lacanian theory of 'the subject'. Any substantive reference to the social formation has been made to disappear. In other words, 'screen theory' poses the problem of the 'politics of the signifier', the struggle over ideology in language, exclusively at the level of 'the subject'.

Against these trenchant criticisms by Stuart Hall and others of 'screen theory' and its use of Lacan's work there are some counter-arguments which should be considered seriously. It is often said that 'screen theory' is anti-humanist in that it deals with structures at the expense of the human. But the counter-argument is that the category of 'the subject' had disappeared in accounts of social structures and that this new work interrogates what hitherto had remained hidden. Why is it so often assumed that a work cannot be marxist because it deals with the subjective?

In Althusser, the reconciliation of the discoveries of Marx and Freud does not take place; they are marked as parallel, both orientated around a 'decentredeness'. Now, Lacan's reading of Freud provides an account of the subjective moment of the social process, the notion that a person and his/her unconscious is formed by his/her history in society and that this formation, particularly the unconscious, can operate according to its own logic and come into conflict with economic needs.

Another common criticism is that structuralism/semiology deals with the synchronic and that recent developments are incapable of dealing with process, transformation or change (the diachronic). But this is countered by the argument that Barthes, Kristeva and Lacan have attempted for many years to dissolve the synchrony/diachrony distinction.

To conclude: though Marx provides no theory of the constitution of the individual, there is nevertheless space in his work for such a theory. Many marxists argue that Lacanian theory — though phallocentric — can fill that space. But any theory of the individual subject must be integrated with historical materialism and must be compatible with Marx's account of the subject of history: social classes. In Lacanian theory the subject is undifferentiated, identical for all human individuals in any society. This theory, therefore, cannot be a candidate, for it contains no reference to social class and the social relations of production.

In spite of these objections to Lacanian theory I want to say that psychoanalysis (because of its emphasis on the neglected areas of desire, repression and wish fulfilment) is very important. Freud and Marx cannot be easily integrated, and attempts to do so have so far been disappointing. Nevertheless the project of attempting to construct a marxist theory of the subjective is a vital one. After all, ideology is not just a system of ideas or a socializing force, but the practice that constructs what is often taken as given, that is, human nature. Ideology is a force that enters into the very constitution of the individual and is therefore the area in which changes of attitudes are generated. I want to suggest that any analysis which separates the subjective and the objective is inadequate. To think the objective without the subjective is to leave the subjective free to reproduce the same old orientations.

Chapter 7

The Post-Structuralism of Foucault

It has been argued so far that a 'Copernican revolution' is taking place, which is undermining traditional ways of perceiving the world. During the last few years there has been a disenchantment with the pragmatic, empirical nature of Anglo-Saxon thought and a swing away from positivistic, quantitative approaches. At the same time there is a great and growing interest in post-structuralist thinkers like Derrida, Lacan and Foucault, who are having a decisive influence in the human sciences. The most well-known of these theorists is probably Michel Foucault. After giving some reasons why his work should be studied, I provide an account of his main works and then focus on the concepts 'knowledge' and 'power'.

Introduction

Michel Foucault, Professor of the History of Systems of Thought at the Collège de France, is exerting an enormous influence on British and American intellectuals. He is an interesting figure: he rejects both Sartrean phenomenology and marxism; he denies being a structuralist. He is fascinated by western rationalism, but his heroes are those who like Nietzsche transgress the rules of Reason. I believe Foucault's work is of great importance to students of the social sciences and education for the following reasons.

1 One of his main concerns is knowledge; he investigates how different disciplines and discourses are constituted. His aim is to uncover the underlying set of rules governing the production of discourses in any single period.

2 Foucault always looks at specific conditions, the ways in which forms of knowledge emerge. He always begins with an

account of what people do. Moreover, in his writings he often refers to the education system and to schools.

3 He poses many provocative questions concerning the birth of modern rationality. His work suggests, for example, that we have not progressed from the dark to the light, but that there has been merely a change in the modalities of control. And so he asks: what will be the consequences of the West's will to knowledge which is also a will to power?

4 Foucault has had considerable influence recently amongst feminists and those concerned with sexual politics because of his stress on what he calls the 'micropolitics of the body'. 'Power sweeps into the very grain of individuals, reaches right into their bodies, permeates their gestures, their posture, what they say, how they learn to live and work with other people.'[1] Foucault rejects functionalism, essentialism, all that is 'pre-given'. He has attempted to lay bare the mechanisms of control and has put forward a new conceptualization of power.

This new theory is influencing the policy and the activities of some political groups and is leading to new definitions and practices of struggle. The effect of this theory and practice on 'classical' marxism will be discussed in the last chapter of the book.

The Human Subject, History and Marxism

In this section I will outline some of the main features of Foucault's work, his views on the status and role of the human subject, the history of ideas, and on marxism.

All of Foucault's works revolve around a single problem: the status and role of the human subject, the concept of human beings in history and in the 'human sciences'. Foucault shares with the structuralists a desire to displace the human subject and its consciousness from the centre of theoretical concern — a position it has enjoyed in French philosophy during the 300 years between Descartes and Sartre.

Foucault has argued that Marx's analysis sought to show that all human activities are in the final analysis determined *outside* the consciousness of the individual subject. After Marx another blow at humanism was dealt by Nietzsche's genealogy, which traced the 'purest' human morality back to the most naked of power struggles.

Since then, psychoanalysis, linguistics and anthropology have decentred the human subject in relation to the laws of desire, the forms of language, and the rules of beliefs and practices.[2] Like the structuralists Foucault rejects the philosophy of the subject, which was why he was taken to be one of them. But it should be stressed that, though he has an 'anti-humanist' position, he is not a structuralist and is not interested in extending the application of the concepts and methods of structural linguistics.

Nor is Foucault interested in history as it is conventionally understood, or in the history of ideas. He has spent a lot of time and energy undermining the preconceptions and methods of the history of ideas. For Foucault history, and the history of ideas in particular, is too deeply imbued with notions of continuity, causality and teleology which stem from modern rationalism and ultimately from the Cartesian notion of the constitutive subject. It was to distinguish what he was doing from the history of ideas that he coined the term 'archeology of knowledge'.

But Foucault is not interested in 'history' for its own sake. His essential concern has always been to understand the present, the present as a product of the past and as the seed-bed of the new. His whole work has been an examination of the nature of historical change; he offers us not a social history, but a history of the social. One would have thought that marxism would have been an important element in such a study, but this is not the case. Though he has shown respect for Marx himself, he has never ceased to question the usefulness of historical materialism.

In Foucault's view, Marx's analysis does not represent a fundamental rupture with previous views of society and history: 'At the deepest level of Western knowledge, Marxism introduced no real discontinuity, it found its place without difficulty.... Marxism exists in nineteenth century thought like a fish in water: that is, it is unable to breathe anywhere else.'[3] He argues that the true epistemic break occurs with the work of David Ricardo, the real founder of modern political economy, and *not* Marx.

Ricardo pointed out that labour could not be used as a constant measure (as Adam Smith had thought). The productive activity of labour was not the measure of value but the source of value. Ricardo freed labour from its role as constant measure of value by placing it prior to all exchange. In short, Foucault implies in his writings that marxist thought is irremediably confined by an episteme that is coming to an end, and that it is anachronistic at this time to call oneself a marxist.

The philosopher that Foucault greatly admires is Nietzsche. Nietzsche plays a central role in Foucault's *Madness and Civilization* as the great mediator between Reason and Unreason. Foucault's concepts 'genealogy' and 'will to knowledge' both derive from Nietzsche. In a revealing interview Foucault writes, 'It was Nietzsche who specified the power relation as the general focus, shall we say, of philosophical discourse — whereas for Marx it was the production relation. Nietzsche is the philosopher of power, but he managed to think power without confining himself within a political theory to do so.'[4]

The Main Works

Foucault's main works show the wide range of his intellectual interests: the history of madness, the emergence of medicine, the nature of discourse, the birth of the prison and the construction of sexuality.

Madness and Civilization is a detailed account of the changes that have occurred in western Europe's view and treatment of insanity over a period of some 300 years.[5] It is a book about the constitution of madness as a mental illness. Foucault suggests that madness was not initially a fact, but a judgement, a judgement passed by one part of the human mind, by one person on another. With the waning of the Middle Ages leprosy disappeared from the western world. Its role as focus of exclusion in the European consciousness was taken over by venereal disease. Then, 200 years later, after a period of latency, madness aroused similar reactions of isolation, exclusion and purification.

The Renaissance expressed its fear of madness (and its fascination with the secret knowledge that madness was believed to conceal) in the works of its painters: Bosch, Dürer, Grunewald and Brueghel. As there was a great fear of the insane, they had to be isolated. Of course human beings did not wait until the seventeenth century to 'shut up' the mad, but it was in this period that they began to 'confine' them, along with an entire population with whom their kinship was recognized. The sudden massive resort to confinement in the mid-seventeenth century was not a necessary response to a sudden massive upsurge of 'asocial elements'. Rather the 'asocial elements' were produced by the act of segregation.

The doctrine of confinement was based on the concept of unreason. Insanity was a consequence rather than a cause of unreasonable behaviour. Madness was perceived as a relapse into animality, the non-human. It was above all the family that requested and obtained a confinement. The family and its demands became one of the essential criteria of reason. During the whole period of the confinement the family was a matter of public concern and whoever attacked it was considered a threat. The principal thesis of *Madness and Civilization* is that reason banished unreason in order to set up its own undivided rule, and that the ascendency of reason brought with it a certain impoverishment of human experience. Foucault argues that the categories of modern psychiatry were produced by that 'science' in its very act of formation.

In his next book, *The Birth of the Clinic*, he focusses on the emergence of another discourse: the rise of clinical medicine during the last years of the eighteenth century when the old classificatory medicine gave way to the clinical method, to medicine as the 'science' we know today. Doctors were able to see and describe what for centuries had lain beneath the level of the visible and the expressible. It was not so much that doctors suddenly opened their eyes; rather that the old codes of knowledge had determined what was seen. Doctors had to transgress and transform the codes they had previously taken for granted.[6] The change was made possible by a complex set of events, a simultaneous change in seeing and saying. It seems to have been achieved by a convergence of the requirements of a political ideology and those of a medical technology. In a concerted effort doctors and statesmen demanded, in a different vocabulary but for identical reasons, the suppression of every obstacle to the constitution of the new medicine. Foucault points out that medicine was of great importance in the formation of the social sciences in that it concerned human beings not only methodologically but also ontologically, as objects of knowledge.

Foucault continues to examine the continuities and transformations in European thought from the Renaissance to the present in *The Order of Things*,[7] in which he focusses on three essential areas concerned respectively with living beings, language and wealth. In his view the naturalists, grammarians and economists of the eighteenth century employed the same rules to define the objects proper to their study, to form their concepts, and to build their theories. This 'archaeological' level consists of a set of rules of formation that determine the conditions of all that can be said within the particular discourse at any given time. General grammar, natural history and the analysis of wealth were sciences of order in the domain of words, beings and needs.

At the end of the eighteenth century there was a far-reaching change in the foundations of knowledge. The eighteenth-century discourses of natural history, general grammar and analysis of wealth became in the nineteenth century biology, philology and political economy. The world is now seen to be made up not of isolated elements, related by identity and difference, but of organic structures, of internal relations between elements whose totality performs a function. Foucault explains:

> Historians want to write histories of biology in the eighteenth century, but they do not realize that biology did not exist then, and that the pattern of knowledge that has been familiar to us for a hundred and fifty years is not valid for a previous period. And that, if biology was unknown, there was a very simple reason for it: that life itself did not exist. All that existed were living beings, which were viewed through a grid of knowledge constituted by *natural history*.[8]

And just as there is no biology or philology in the classical period, so there is no political economy in the sense (understood since Ricardo) of a discipline based on the concept of production. Similarly, in classical thought, language as a problem did not exist, because it was at once ubiquitous and transparent, so man, as an object of knowledge, did not exist. Human beings, as objects of scientific knowledge, make their appearance when language ceases to be the unquestioned universal model of knowledge, when language becomes opaque and problematic. 'Man' as an operational concept emerges through the development of biology, political economy, and philology.

Discourse and the 'Will to Knowledge'

Foucault often uses the term 'discourse'. In *The Archaeology of Knowledge* he tells us that the object of a discourse is not to be confused with what linguists call the referent (the actual thing referred to by a verbal sign). Discourse is not about objects; rather discourse constitutes them. Discourses, writes Foucault, are 'practices that systematically form the objects of which they speak. Of course, discourses are composed of signs; but what they do is more than use these signs to designate things. It is this *more* that renders them irreducible to the language [*langue*] and to speech.'[9]

Foucault has described some of the procedures that control

discourse. Firstly, there is prohibition: we know very well that we are not free to say anything, that we cannot speak of anything when and where we like. The second principle of exclusion is that of revision and rejection, for example, the discourse of the 'mad' person is not treated in the same way as that of a 'normal' person. Thirdly, there is the opposition between the true and the false.

Another group of procedures for the control of discourse includes systems of restriction like ritual: the qualifications required of the speaking subject, the gestures, the behaviour, the signs that must accompany the discourse. Then there are 'societies of discourse', whose function is to preserve discourse by producing it in a restricted group. Foucault is aware that there are great differences in the 'social appropriation' of discourse. An education system is a means of qualifying the speaking subjects, the constitution of a doctrinal group, a distribution and an appropriation of discourse:

> But we know very well that, in its distribution, in what it permits and what it prevents, it follows the lines laid down by social differences, conflicts and struggles. Every educational system is a political means of maintaining or modifying the appropriation of discourses, with the knowledge and power they bring with them.[10]

It is the 'will to knowledge' that creates new arrangements of the objects to be studied. There is a whole institutional base on which the will to truth operates: the educational system, libraries, laboratories, learned societies, the values set by different social systems on different forms of knowledge. The will to knowledge has deeply marked the whole of western civilization over the last 2500 years:

> The historical analysis of this rancorous will to knowledge reveals that all knowledge rests upon injustice ... and that the instinct for knowledge is malicious (something murderous, opposed to the happiness of mankind).... The desire for knowledge has been transformed among us into a passion which fears no sacrifice, which fears nothing but its own extinction. It may be that mankind may eventually perish from this passion for knowledge.[11]

Schools and the New Technology of Subjection

Foucault eloquently argues that the forms of power in society are imbued with social and psychological knowledge, but equally those forms of knowledge are permeated by power relations. The exercise of power over the population and the accumulation of knowledge about it are two sides of a single process: not power and knowledge, but power-knowledge. These ideas are clearly expressed in *Discipline and Punish, the Birth of the Prison*. In this book Foucault shows how the still largely 'medieval' penal theory and practice of the *ancien régime* gave way in France, after the Revolution, to an institutionalization of imprisonment on quite different theoretical premises.[12] He shows that the techniques of discipline and observation incorporated in the new prison derive from three centuries of practice in other spheres, notably in education and the army. Moreover, there is an astonishing coincidence between the new prison and other contemporary institutions: the hospital, factory, school, and barracks.

The courts became less and less concerned with punishment, more and more with correction and reclamation. The judgement of offences became more and more supplemented, even supplanted, by knowledge of the offender. A whole set of assessing, diagnostic, prognostic, normative judgements concerning the individual became the norm. This shift away from overt punishment of the body to investigation of the prisoner's 'soul' can only be understood by seeing the new penal methods and the social sciences that provide the 'knowledge' on which these methods are based as having a common origin: the growth of power-knowledge.

Foucault outlines the conditions required for the implementation of discipline. First, discipline is cellular. In the schools, for example, the boarders not only slept in cells under constant supervision, but their daytime activities were dictated by a cellular system of grading according to age and ability. The educational space functioned like a learning machine that also supervised, hierarchized, rewarded and punished. Secondly, the disciplines initiated a control of activity. The chief mechanism for this was the timetable. Regularity and rhythm were applied not only to the individual's general activities, but also to the very movements of the body. Thirdly, discipline was imposed upon the body in a temporal sense: the process of training could be broken down into stages with a view to the development of ever greater skills. Foucault emphasizes that the eighteenth century saw a great increase in attention paid to the body as object and target of power, an instrument that could be trained and manipulated, whose forces could be extracted and increased. All these disciplinary procedures combined to produce a totally rational, efficient and controlled society.

Architecture played an important part in this process. A new kind of architecture developed which was based on Bentham's 'panopticon', a system in which the inmate of each cell is in full view of the central observer, himself unseen. The inmate never knows when he is being observed and therefore behaves at all times as if he were. The 'panopticon' was a mechanism of power adaptable to any enclosed institution. In schools it made it possible to observe performances, to map attitudes, to assess characters.[13] The techniques of hierarchical observation and normalizing judgement combine in the examination. The knowledge extracted from the various forms of examination is committed to writing in the form of reports and files. Thus coercive, centralized normality is imposed on education.

In short, Foucault describes how the traditional, ritual, costly, violent forms of power were superseded by a subtle, calculated technology of subjection; how power became more anonymous and more functional. Now, it is generally agreed that prisons do not diminish the crime rate; detention causes recidivism, the prison indirectly produces criminals. But, if this is the case, why is it allowed to continue? The prison and the legal system generally is to be understood as a means not of eliminating crime, but rather of differentiating between types of crimes, types of criminals, setting one potential source of social instability against another, using one against the other.

Prisons have created an autonomous subclass of delinquents. By concentrating in one relatively small group the illegalities that threatened to infect the mass of the population, it was possible to contain them. The establishment of a class of delinquents as a kind of enclosed illegality has a number of advantages. It is possible to supervise illegality and to divert it to forms of illegalities that are politically harmless and economically negligible. In fact this concentrated, supervised and disarmed illegality is directly useful. *It provides a justification and a means for the general surveillance, for the policing of the entire population.*

One of Foucault's main concerns, then, is to show how society increasingly developed mechanisms in the nineteenth century for policing the individual's behaviour. The state even had to know what was happening with its citizens' sex; it was necessary to know about health, fertility, life expectancy, birth and death rates. The sexuality of school children was of paramount interest to all those concerned with education. Later, medicine and psychiatry turned to sex and took over its management.

Foucault suggests in *The History of Sexuality* that there have been two main approaches to sex.[14] *Ars erotica*, in India, China and

Japan, entails that knowledge is kept secret and is handed down from master to disciple. In western culture there is a *scientia sexualis* which is based on a form of power-knowledge, namely the confession. In the eastern initiatory tradition the revelation of truth comes from above, from the master who passes it on to the disciple. In the western confessional tradition truth rises from below, from the penitent, offender or patient and is received and used by the authority figure: 'The confession has spread its effects far and wide. It plays a part in law, medicine, education, family relationships, and sexual relations, in ordinary, everyday matters and in the most solemn rites ... one confesses in public and in private, to one's parents, to one's teachers....'[15]

Foucault shows how sex became an object of scientific discourse and practice. There developed an all-pervasive sexualization of illness. The slightest sexual defect or deviation was thought to possess untold consequences in terms of health and sanity. Foucault is, however, a strong critic of the so-called 'repressive' theory. He points out that if the purpose of sexual repression was a more intensive use of the labour force, one would expect that the machinery of repression would have been directed above all at the working class, in particular the young, adult male. This was not the case.

Since the seventeenth century the new form of power over life has operated in two principal ways. First, *the body has been treated like a machine*, its capacities extended, its performance improved, its power extracted. The second, which developed about a century later in the mid-eighteenth century, was centred on the body as a species, a regulation of the population in terms of birth and death rates, health levels, life expectancies. This two-sided technology — anatomical and biological — penetrated life in an ever more thorough manner. Sex, then, as a political issue forms a hinge between the disciplines of the body and the regulation of populations. It gave rise to minute surveillances, unceasing controls — a whole micro-power over the body. But it also gave rise to measures on a massive scale, statistical calculations, interventions in societies as a whole.

Power-Knowledge

Foucault thus forces us to reconsider the relations between knowledge and power. Knowledge does not 'reflect' power relations; it is not a distorted expression of them; it is immanent in them: 'Power produces knowledge.... Power and knowledge directly imply one another.... There is no power relation without the correlative constitution of a field of knowledge, nor any knowledge that does not presuppose and constitute at the same time power relations.'[16]

Power and knowledge are two sides of the same process. Knowledge cannot be neutral, pure. All knowledge is political not because it may have political consequences or be politically useful, but because knowledge has its conditions of possibility in power relations. Knowledge is not so much true or false as legitimate or illegitimate for a particular set of power relations. Foucault shows that truth does not exist outside power, still less in opposition to it. Each society has its own 'régime of truth' (that is, what can be said and what must be left unsaid), its types of discourse accepted as true, and the mechanisms that make it possible to distinguish between truth and error.

But what does Foucault mean by power? He does not think of power in the sense of a unified state apparatus whose task is to ensure the subjection of the citizens of a particular society. Nor does he mean a general system of domination exerted by one group over another, the effect of which spreads to the whole society. Power should be understood as 'the multiplicity of power relations' at work in a particular area. Power does not reside in some primary, central point. Power is ubiquitous because it is produced at every moment: 'Power is everywhere ... power is not an institution, nor a structure, nor a possession. It is a name we give to a complex strategic situation in a particular society.'[17]

Power is not something that can be acquired, seized, or shared. It is *exercised* from innumerable points, in a set of unequal, shifting relations. Power relations do not exist outside other types of relation (for example, those found in economic processes, in the diffusion of knowledge, in sexual relations), but are immanent in them. Power relations are not a matter of a totally binary opposition between dominators and dominated, which is then reproduced from top to bottom in ever smaller groupings, but are formed and operate in places of work, families, institutions, groups of all kinds, etc. There is a general line of force that traverses local confrontations and links them together; in turn, the local confrontations reverberate back through the series thus created to effect new alignments, new conflicts.

Foucault's conception of power constitutes a radical break with all previous conceptions of power. He argues that power is not a possession won by one class that strives to retain it against its acquisition by another. Power is not the prerogative of a dominant class which exercises it actively upon a passive, dominated class, and the working class has no historical mission in acquiring it. He even suggests that it is unhelpful to think in terms of 'classes' in this way, for power is not unitary. Power is an effect of the operation of social relationships between groups and between individuals. There are as many forms of power as there are types of relationship. Every group and every individual exercises power and is subjected to it. The ability of certain categories of people — children, prisoners, the insane — to exercise power is severely limited; nevertheless most members of these groups find some means of exercising it, if only on each other.

Power, then, is not to be identified with the state, a central apparatus that can be seized. The state is rather an overall strategy and effect, a composite result made up of a multiplicity of centres and mechanisms, so many states within states with complex networks of common citizenship. Factories, housing estates, hospitals, families, schools are among the more evident of the 'micro-powers', the network of power relations that permeate every aspect of social life. For that reason 'power' cannot be overthrown and acquired once and for all by the destruction of institutions and the seizure of the state apparatuses. Because power is multiple and ubiquitous, the struggle against it must be localized. Equally, however, because it is a network and not a collection of isolated points, each localized struggle induces effects on the entire network. Struggle, therefore, cannot be totalized; a single centralized, hierarchical organization setting out to seize a single centralized, hierarchical power is not possible. Struggle can, however, be *serial*, that is, in terms of horizontal links between one point of struggle and another.

To sum up this section: Foucault's approach is concerned with showing how a particular administration has come about, how certain discourses and practices have created a disciplinary society. Foucault is very critical of two taken-for-granted ideas: knowledge and power. He argues against those who believe that knowledge, at present held by the bourgeoisie, can be simply taken over by the proletariat. In his view knowledge is not just a neutral tool; knowledge is always interconnected with power.

Moreover, Foucault argues that power is not a possession of a class, but permeates society and all its interrelations. In short, Foucault suggests that it is pointless to ask epistemological questions; we should, instead, focus on how discourses are produced and how they produce 'normalized' individuals. Intellectuals, as we shall see, play an important part in this process.[18] Discourses and practices mesh together to produce social administration; they have the power to produce docile individuals.

Foucault contends that the intelligibility of power relations is not to be found in terms of causality, of events at one level causing or explaining events on another, but rather in a series of aims and objectives. However, these are not attributable to an individual subject, not even to a ruling caste, but arise in an apparently anonymous way from the local situations in which they first appear. Where there is power there is resistance; power relations depend on a multiplicity of points of resistance, which serve at once as adversary, target, support, foothold.

Just as there is no centre of power, there is no centre of revolt, from which secondary rebellions derive, no unified class that is the seat of rebellion. There is a plurality of resistances, each a special case, distributed in an irregular way in time and space. Sometimes a broad series of resistances converges to bring about a major upheaval, a 'revolution', but like power, and inextricably linked with it, resistance takes the form of innumerable, mobile, transitory points.

A Foucaldian Approach in the Psychology of Education

Now that I have outlined Foucault's key concepts and given an exposition of his main books I will relate his approach to some ongoing work in education to show its relevance. Though I am sceptical of some aspects of Foucault's work — I will state my criticisms at the end of the chapter — I should make it clear that some social scientists have found his approach very useful. Some thought-provoking work is beginning to be done in the psychology of education, utilizing the insights of Foucault.

Many progressive intellectuals assert that psychology, for example, is bourgeois, and they then proceed to leave the discipline. But it could be argued that this is an inadequate strategy and that a Foucaldian approach would be more constructive. Let us consider an example of this approach from developmental psychology, which has been used to reveal the 'history of the social', the present.

In an interesting article Valerie Walkerdine has focussed upon the relationship between the psychology of child development and progressive education.[19] Both emerged at the same time, but what function did the relation between child development and progressive education have? The early pioneers of education, Maria Montessori, Susan Isaacs and others, monitored experiments with children.[20] And then there was the timely discovery by Jean Piaget of intellectual development as a universal sequence of mental stages.[21] What is the link between developmental psychology and progressive education?

The author suggests that during the 1920s and 1930s many educationalists feared that it was the regimentation of schools that had helped to produce in the personalities of people those traits which had fuelled totalitarianism in Italy, Germany and Russia. A widely-held belief at that time was that anti-social degeneracy was produced by over-regulated practices. Rationality unfolded 'naturally'. As a consequence, there was an emphasis on 'setting the children free'. Psychoanalytic theory, which stressed the harmful aspects of repression, provided a rationale for such freedom.[22] Progressive education would, it was felt, leave children free of regimentation while ensuring by means of close and detailed observation that children were not developing undesirable characteristics. It was in this social and political context that Jean Piaget produced a stage-theory of development which fitted the need for a 'scientific pedagogy'.

Many educationalists began to open progressive schools where the emphasis was on experience and discovery, the use of concrete objects, play as a means of learning. Dora Russell's school at Beacon Hill and A.S. Neill's Summerhill, for example, emphasized freedom as a reaction against the totalitarianism of the Right, but there were others who stressed freedom as a bulwark against the authoritarian Left. Another pioneer of progressive education was Homer Lane who founded 'the Little Commonwealth'. Here it was assumed that children became rational 'naturally' without adult intervention. In this view democracy was a natural phenomenon. Although some of this early work was privately funded, it was not long before 'Progressive Education' began to get the backing of those in charge of public education.

Valerie Walkerdine argues that the theories of Piaget provided a pedagogy for a covert administration that had the *appearance* of setting the children free. Gradually, many of these discourses have come to be seen as 'commonsense'. Many Piagetian assumptions, such as 'children develop at their own rate', are now taken for granted by teachers. It is not sufficiently realized that we regard many of our assumptions as 'facts' rather than theoretical concepts which have been historically produced. According to the Foucaldian approach taken-for-granted assumptions should be challenged and subverted.[23]

Let me give another example. Intelligence testing is often seen as reactionary, and many radicals reject it; nevertheless this rejection leaves grading and hierarchizing to carry on as before. A more constructive approach would be to ask: how was this discourse produced? Nikolas Rose has written about how the discourse of psychology developed a connected 'régime of truth' in the nineteenth century.[24] New categorizations were constructed: 'races', 'children', 'patients', 'criminals'. Crime, pauperism and inefficiency were blamed on 'high-grade defectives' and a testing instrument developed. Galton, Terman, Binet and others produced numerous tests. It can be shown that the concept of 'feeblemindedness' did not exist before the category was invented, but once the category was established, the act of classification, the practice, had important effects. This is, after all, what Foucault means by discourse — a practice that constitutes the object of which it speaks.

Some Criticisms of Foucault's Work

In his critique of particular variants of marxism Foucault insists that the conditions of possibility for the emergence of a particular discursive practice, together with the power relations which are integral to it, are not derived from any single or primary cause. He is highly critical of the construction and use of any general theoretical or universalist concepts and insists on historical specificity at all levels.

Though there are certain real advantages to be gained from the use of Foucault's approach in historically specific analyses, there are some criticisms that must be made. Foucault rejects what he calls 'global theories of history', those theories which attempt to give a total description of historical reality, including the history of ideas, ideologies and science. He does not like explanations which rely on a single, dominating principle, meaning or cause.

Foucault not only rejects the marxist theory of ideology, which he believes to be reductionist, but he also abandons class analysis. He is unwilling, therefore, to treat mass schooling as an instrument of class domination. In his preoccupation with the technological features of disciplinary power he systematically ignores that these techniques are applied precisely to ensure the reproduction of the social relations of the capitalist mode of production. In Foucault's work power relations are severed from an understanding of class domination and the state as a political form of the rule of capital. Power is thought of in terms of institutional functions. Power becomes ultimately co-extensive with social structure and ceases to have any explanatory capacity as a concept.

Power, Foucault contends, is not to be identified with the state, a central, unified entity that can be seized. Whilst I would agree that the system is not unified, I cannot agree with those who say that there is no state apparatus or that 'the state is everywhere'. According to Foucault, as the unified state does not exist, it cannot be seized. Such a conception leads to a view which finds a central directing party redundant.

It is often claimed that Foucault's anti-authoritarianism, his rejection of any central, organizing entity, such as the state or party, offers a new basis for the diverse and decentred struggles not only of women, but of black people, prisoners, mental patients, welfare recipients, factory workers and so forth, against the particular manifestations of disciplinary power in their respective arenas. The rejection of the concept 'class' has allowed a segment of the Women's Liberation Movement to justify involvement in a struggle outside a marxist framework. The conflict thus focusses not on the antagonism of the proletariat against the bourgeoisie, but of women against men. Indeed, it is quite remarkable how many similarities there are between Foucault's thesis about power, with its abandonment of class analysis, and traditional American sociology, which depicted a world in which power is diffuse and fragmented and where there is a plurality of competing 'interest groups'.

In my opinion Foucault is often vague and ambiguous because he gives no account of material determinations. There is no analysis of capital. He ignores the fact that the exercise of power depends on material conditions existing independently of it.[25] One of the main problems of Foucault's work is that discourses/practices seem to be virtually independent of the production process, of class struggle, of politics. Prisons, hospitals, schools emerge as structures of statements. Power appears as a function not of classes, not of the state, but of discourse itself. Indeed, Foucault says that his own work is to be regarded as 'a discourse about discourse'. Wherever Foucault looks, he finds nothing but discourse.

In short, Foucault not only rejects class analysis, which attempts to derive existing forms of power from the productive relations of capitalist society; he also repudiates the concepts of ideology, state and party. The Foucaldian approach, though it produces very interesting work (from which I have learned a lot), puts into question many categories that marxists take for granted.

Chapter 8

The Family, State and Schooling

I now want to illustrate some of the themes mentioned in the last chapter by reviewing Jacques Donzelot's book *The Policing of Families*.[1] Donzelot, whose mentor is Foucault, shares the same theoretical assumptions and concerns as Foucault. Both are interested not in social history but in the history of the 'social'; both focus on how the social sciences have become disciplines of control and surveillance of the population.

Foucault has written how the family is simultaneously defined as the normal human unit and as the battleground between men and women, young and old, parents and children, and, by extension, teachers and students, priests and laymen, rulers and ruled.[2] Donzelot's book is about the advent of the modern family and the place of children within it. As the book describes the social construction of different models of childhood and the increasing power of social workers and child psychiatrists, it has a particular relevance for teachers.[3] At the end of the chapter I will relate what Foucault and Donzelot are saying about the increase in social control, order and efficiency to what is happening in the educational system.

The Advent of the Modern Family

Donzelot argues that the modern sense of the family emerged in the bourgeois and aristocratic strata of the *ancien régime*, then spread in concentric circles to all social classes, reaching the proletariat at the end of the nineteenth century. According to his research, many books began to be written on the theme of the preservation of children in the middle of the eighteenth century. These books attacked the practice of foundling hospitals, the rearing of children by domestic nurses, and the 'artificial' education of rich children. It was said that

these techniques impoverished the nation. For example, the administration of foundling children was reproached for appalling mortality
rates of the minors in its care — children that could have been useful
to the state in its militia or its policies of colonization. The education
of rich children suffered from being left up to house servants who
treated them to a mixture of constraints and liberties, unsuited to
their development, as was shown by the use of swaddling clothes.

Donzelot goes on to state that in the nineteenth century an
alliance was formed between doctors and mothers, which favoured
the advancement of women by the recognition of their educative
usefulness. Moreover, it enabled doctors to attack the old structures
of education and religious discipline and to establish family medicine.
This was an alliance profitable to both parties: with the mother's help
the doctor prevailed against the popular medicine of the 'old wives',
and on the other hand he conceded a new power to the bourgeois
woman in the domestic sphere. It was this promotion of the woman
as mother, educator, and a medical auxiliary that was to serve as a
point of support for the main feminist currents of the nineteenth
century.

As to the lower classes, the abandonment of children in hospital
sanctuaries was discarded and a system of aid to mothers at home was
instituted. But this aid was based on an administrative investigation of
the mother's situation. There was also an extension of medical control
over the rearing of children from working-class families.

In fact, a multitude of philanthropic and religious associations
had made it their goal to come to the aid of the poorer classes, to
moralize their behaviour and facilitate their education by concentrating their efforts towards the restoration of family life. Many of the
religious societies made the marriage contract a condition for benefit-
ing from its aid. This strategy of familializing the popular strata rested
mainly on the woman. She was given a new weapon: low-rent
housing. The housing was granted on conditions of eligibility that
guaranteed the morality of the occupants. If they transgressed the
conditions, they were dispossessed. Thus the workers' adherence to
public order was ensured by their desire to keep their housing unit.
The problem was to organize a space large enough to be hygienic,
small enough so that only the family could live in it (no lodgers), and
arranged in such a way that the parents could monitor their children.
The objective was the separation of the sexes and ages within
workers' housing.

In short, the advent of the modern family was constituted by the
woman's alliance with the doctor, which reinforced her internal

authority. Owing to the revalorization of educative tasks, a new continuity was established for the bourgeois woman between her family activities and her social activities. The bourgeois family gradually came to resemble a hothouse insulated from outside influences. A sanitary cordon was drawn around the child; inside the perimeter the growth of his body and mind would be encouraged. This model of childhood can be called *protected liberation*. On the other hand, the working-class family was dispossessed, exposed to the surveillance of its deviations from the norm. The pedagogical model for the working-class child was *supervised freedom*. Instead of being left to the street the child had to be more closely watched in the family dwelling or the school.

From Charity to Philanthropy

The main problems in the first half of the nineteenth century were the deep social divisions and pauperism. The government was obliged to choose between institutionalization of charity, which sanctioned aid as a right, and a violent repression of the poor. The possibility of a repression of the poor as a solution to the problems they posed diminished with their entry onto the political stage. How, then, was it possible to preserve and shape the population and yet dominate, pacify and integrate it? The answer was: philanthropy.

This was a deliberate depoliticizing strategy for establishing public service and facilities midway between private initiative and the state. The old form of charity was displaced in favour of philanthropic benevolence. This strategy involved new forms of power: effective advice rather than humiliating charity, the preserving norm rather than destructive repression. Philanthropy differed from charity — there was an emphasis on advice instead of gifts, assistance to children rather than old people, and to women rather than men. The granting of assistance, however, was conditional on an investigation of needs by probing into the moral life of the poor recipient.

A key question of the time was the adult-child relationship. From the 1840s to the end of the nineteenth century a large number of bills were enacted to protect children. The object of these measures was hygienic and political in nature. They sought 'to reduce the sociopolitical capacity of these strata by breaking the initiatory ties that existed between children and adults, the autarchic transmission of skills, the freedom of movement and of agitation that resulted from the loosening of the ancient communal constraints.'[4]

The struggle of the philanthropists against the abandonment and exploitation of children was also a struggle against those enclaves that allowed for autonomous ties between the generations and, consequently, against what resulted politically: a moving force that was unpredictable and uncontrollable, the pre-industrial masses who produced the great revolts of the nineteenth century.

Government through the Family

The many organizations that were interested in preventing crimes *against children* could also penetrate into families from the angle of violations committed *by children*. Thus, at the end of the nineteenth century assistance to the abandoned and repression of family rebels were combined. It became legitimate to acknowledge the public usefulness of social housing, schools, savings-banks, family allowances, of all the services and facilities set up by employers anxious to contain the poor, since these instruments of moralization were also necessary to a healthy society.

A result of these tendencies was a reduction of family autonomy, a reduction that was facilitated by the appearance of a whole series of connections between public assistance, juvenile law, medicine, and psychiatry:

> By this bringing together, under the theme of prevention, the formerly separate activities of assistance and repression, the care and custody of children without families and of rebels against the family, one stripped the latter of its long-standing position of interlocutor, one reversed the relationship of collusion between the state and the family, making the family a sphere of direct intervention, a missionary field.[5]

In other words, there was a transition from a government of families to a government through the family. The protection of poor children allowed for the destruction of the family as an island of resistance; the privileged alliance of the doctor and the educator developed procedures of savings, educational promotion, and so on. The family, then, was a perfect method of social control; there was a renunciation of the question of political right through the private pursuit of well-being. In a sense the modern family is not so much an institution as a mechanism.

The Emergence of Social Work and Child Psychiatry

Since the end of the nineteenth century a new series of professions has appeared which are all concerned with social work. Indeed, it could be said that the social worker is gradually taking over from the teacher in importance. Many social workers focus on the pathology of children in its dual form: children in danger and dangerous children (that is 'delinquents'). Social workers, using psychiatric, sociological and psychoanalytic knowledge for support, hope to forestall police action by replacing the secular arm of the law with the extended hand of the educator.

Donzelot describes a paradoxical result of the liberalization of the family, of the emergence of children's rights, of a rebalancing of the man-woman relationship: the more these rights are proclaimed, the more the strangle-hold of authority tightens around the poor family. And so there is a new relation between the public and the private spheres; as the state finances more, so it controls more. In this system patriarchy in the family is destroyed and replaced by the patriarchy of the state.[6]

At the end of the nineteenth century psychiatrists proposed to go beyond their minor function in the judiciary and achieve an autonomous position as prime movers in the prevention and treatment of delinquency. In a sense this emergence of the psychiatrist was ordered by a summons issuing from two apparatuses in full expansion: the army and the schools. Making education free and compulsory caused the schools to be filled with a mass of children either unwilling to submit to scholastic discipline, or ill prepared for it.

The main concerns of psychiatrists at this time were the hysteric, the mentally defective, and the pervert. For roughly ten years (1890–1900), in France the vagabond became the universal of mental pathology, the prism through which all the categories of madness and abnormality could be distributed. The vagabond displayed to the maximum all the pathological effects of the weaknesses of childhood when they were not corrected or checked in time.

For psychiatrists the schools came to be regarded as a laboratory for the observation of anti-social tendencies. The child's deficiencies could be related in turn to two types of family deficiency: educational insufficiency and the existence of degenerative anomalies. Thus, more than the patient, more than the problem child, the family became the true locus of illness. At the time when juvenile law was being constructed on the basis of the desire to replace punishment with prevention, repression with education, the psychiatrist appeared at the judge's side, motivated by the same project as he, but endowed with a theoretical capacity for assessing the suitability of a particular educative approach.[7]

In Donzelot's view a juvenile court is a visible form of the state as family, of the tutelary society (a society that serves as guardian or protector). The juvenile court does not really pronounce judgement on crimes; it examines individuals. An extra-judicial jurisdiction is made up of educators, psychologists, social workers, psychiatrists, and psychoanalysts. Their job is to draw up a synthesis and supply an expert opinion as to the most appropriate measure to administer to the minor. Here one sees the gradual emergence of three modes of knowledge — inquisitorial, classificatory and interpretative.

Psychoanalysis did not really enter the field of juvenile law until after the Second World War. The judicial apparatus discovered the usefulness of having recourse to a specialist ally in order to re-establish undisputed control over the practices of surveillance. Classical psychiatry had become inadequate to some extent. Whilst the psychiatrists concentrated on the detection of ineducable individuals, the juvenile judges believed in the educability of all minors. In other words, psychiatrists and educators took strictly opposite approaches to the educational process and, consequently, were incapable of reaching an understanding. One difference was that psychiatrists used the term 'pervert' in their diagnoses, but the educators and the psychoanalysts, the educators' new allies, thought that the notion of constitutional perversity implied a hopeless prognosis. Gradually the term 'pervert' was given up.

Before the Second World War books on problem children always employed the label 'abnormal'; later there was the classification 'irregular children', a term which did not sound too medical. Then the term 'irregular' was officially replaced by that of 'infantile maladjustment'. This evolution corresponded to the increasing use of psychoanalysis, which brought in a grid that made it possible to code all categories of children.

In this way the psychiatrist, who had been the judge's rival, now became, with the help of psychoanalysis, his indispensable ally. The psychiatrist placed at the judge's disposition a flexible selecting mechanism for the categorization of minors. 'Poor families knew nothing about this grid of the psychoanalysts which placed them, without defences, in the field of a tutelary complex whose internal boundaries melted away and whose external limit was imperceptible.'[8]

Before making a brief comment on Donzelot's work I would like to reiterate his main thesis. In the middle of the eighteenth century the rich had a bad private economy that prompted them to entrust house servants with the education of their children. With respect to the poor there was a bad public economy that led them to abandon their own children, to desert the rural areas and burden the state with responsibilities.

There was a transformation of the family in the nineteenth century which resulted from a propagation within it of medical, educative and relational norms whose overall aim was to preserve children from the old customs which were considered deadly. The *bourgeois family* seized on medical instructions and used them to free children from the control of domestic servants and social promiscuities, constructing around the child an educative model which Donzelot terms protected liberation. On the other hand, the *working-class family* was reorganized on the basis of a set of institutional constraints that also made the child the centre of the family, but according to what Donzelot has called supervised freedom.

The family was also transformed from without by the modification of family law. By the terms of the new law the monolithic authority of the father gave place to a dual régime, which took the form of a simple alternative: either the system of the contract or that of tutelage.[9]

The contractual system, for the bourgeois family, corresponded to an accelerated liberalization of relations, both within and without the family. Tutelage meant that the families of the lower social categories were stripped of all effective rights and brought into a relation of dependence *vis-à-vis* welfare and educative agents.

According to the foreword by Gilles Deleuze, Donzelot's method is genealogical, functional and yet strategic, which expresses his considerable debt to Foucault. Unfortunately, Deleuze's explanation of the method is impenetrably obscure. In my view this obscurity and the limitations of Donzelot's book stem from the same source — the Foucaldian view of power.

Donzelot does not see the modern family as an ideological apparatus of the capitalist state. Indeed, the 'state' as such seems to play little part in his scenario. There are no references to any developments in the mode of production and to the struggle between social classes. Neither does he allude to ideology. Changes in society seem to be brought about by individuals or occupational groups. Sometimes one even gets the impression that a struggle is being carried out between different, conflicting discourses. And yet the relationship of 'knowledge' to 'power' remains very general and unspecified.

The Policing of Schools

It is not only Foucault and Donzelot who have pointed to the controlling and system-maintenance functions of the modern state. Many socialist critics have said that the provision of state education, for example, reinforces the *status quo* in the interests of order and efficiency. In other words, the intervention of the capitalist state in education is an attempt to stabilize and reinforce the system. The state is defined as the social institution with the primary function of maintaining order and harmony in the relations of production. The mechanisms for carrying out this function include the army, police, courts and schools. In whatever form these aspects of the state's activity are financed, they constitute in essence taxes on capital. That is to say, they are part of the price that capital has to pay for the maintenance of the system.

Now, writers such as Foucault have exposed the police officer, the social worker, the therapist, the guard behind the caring smile of the school teacher. Foucault's work has been used to explain the recent increase in centralized control of the education system. Consider the following facts: the great increase in national monitoring of pupils, the rapid growth of 'corporate management', a form of managerialism emphasizing efficiency.[10] There is also a replacement of teachers' professional judgement by bureaucratic accountability. The old hegemonic value-system has broken down, and there is no consensus on educational goals.[11]

National monitoring of what children are able to do is now a common occurrence. Why is this? Some of the reasons given will be familiar. People are interested in knowing whether standards are going up or down, and so data are required. It is said that, if data were available, many teachers who now feel threatened could actually show that some standards were improving. Secondly, there is the argument that we need to evaluate to see if educational goals are being achieved. Thirdly, it is often suggested that we need to investigate areas of deficiency so that adequate funding can be provided. Indeed, some government departments want data so that political decisions can be made.

One of the key issues in this area is how the *objectives* of the curriculum are to be decided. Are the aims to be derived from the academic experts, the teachers who know the needs of the children, or the outside community? Agreement on objectives is difficult to reach, partly because there are rapid changes in our idea of a discipline (for example, social studies) and of how we conceive the curriculum itself. Moreover, our presuppositions are cultural and therefore not value-free. Of course, objectives can be arrived at by consensus, but a so-called 'neutral' view is often a dominant cultural view. A consensus often disguises real differences and is therefore unsatisfactory.

Another feature of the present situation is that there is an increasing emphasis on how educational knowledge is consumed at the expense of how it is produced. For example, the Schools' Council is being abolished, and there is an increase in the importance of the Assessment and Performance Unit. This reflects the cutting back of the influence of teachers at both classroom and policy levels. All these changes represent a shift towards more coercive control and accountability, tendencies which are being justified by a scapegoating of the educational system for the failures of the capitalist system.[12]

As an example of this shift towards the political Right let us consider for a moment the teaching of sex education. It is interesting to note how the rhetoric of sex education has changed during the last few years. A private subject has now become a public issue. At one time radicals thought that sex education could be utilized for progressive ends, but now the subject is being used to propagate a return to traditional values. 'Post-liberals' and others have made social and moral issues (such as the family and family-related topics) their main platform. The 'New Right' has successfully colonized this area because they stress absolute values about the family and sexual behaviour, thus giving people a feeling of security at a time of rapid social change. It has often been remarked that Thatcherism and Reaganism have similar views not only on the state and the economy, but on state and social policies concerning the family. There is, then, a shift in the curriculum, particularly in sex eduction, education for parenthood, health education, and other courses from an emphasis on 'equal rights' towards conservative, anti-feminist elements. In short, there is a recrudescence of the traditional, patriarchal view of the family and the fixed, subordinate woman's role within it.

It seems to me that Foucault, Donzelot, and other writers like them only look at the social control function, the disciplinary practices that produce 'normalized' individuals. They neglect the 'social liberatory' elements which are inextricably entangled with the coercive ones. Those who see schools as simply a policing operation have to face the following problem: logically, they should support the cuts in educational expenditure, but politically, should they oppose them?[13]

One limitation of the Foucaldian approach, then, is that analysis of schools is limited to their policing function. It is asserted that discipline and schooling attempt to transform children to be docile, productive, hard-working, self-regulating, conscience-ridden, 'normal' in every way. Now, I want to argue that schooling/education combines two functions which are difficult to separate; though it has a social control function, it also provides to some extent a benefit which improves people's quality of life. Whilst teachers are acting as police agents through the exercise of more or less open coercion, or as ideological agents for the transmission of dominant norms and values, they are *also*, sometimes, and in part, making students critically aware, raising their consciousness, doing 'good'. I do believe that teachers should be more aware of the impulse towards totalitarian control, which Foucault and Donzelot conceive to be intrinsic to modern society, but this is not enough. Teachers should come out on the side of their pupils against the authority of those who exercise the power of exclusion. But how is this to be done? What revolutionary strategy is to be adopted? To questions such as these Foucaldians have no viable answer.

I have emphasized the limitations of Foucault's approach because I believe that they are typical and symptomatic of most versions of post-structuralism. The work of many post-structuralists has a tendency towards idealism (Kristeva) and relativism (the constant deferring of meaning in Derrida); its effects include the fragmentation of class politics and an emphasis on interest groups (Foucault), the deconstruction of classical marxism itself (Hindess and Hirst) and the acceptance of a reformist social democratic strategy. Against the theoreticist idealism of the post-structuralists I want to assert the value and relevance of a marxism that is concerned with what they neglect: social change.

Chapter 9

Teachers: Class Position and Socialist Pedagogy

The Failure of Social Democratic Policies

So that we can better understand some of the problems of social change and the difficulties facing the Left, I want to briefly discuss the Labour Party's post-war education policy. One of the most interesting accounts is the book *Unpopular Education: Schooling and Social Democracy in England since 1944.*[1] It is worth outlining the book's argument at some length because it emphasizes the point that social democratic policies, however well-intentioned, will always fail.

The authors argue that from the 1920s onwards the answer of the Labour Party to the systematic exclusion of the majority of children was to ensure universal access to secondary education. The official programme centred on matters of *access*, and the discussion on educational content, control, and context of schooling was cursory. Labour Party policy embraced both an educational egalitarianism and a more meritocratic concern with 'equality of opportunity'. It is this combination, the attempt to serve popular interests in a socialist or democratic form *and* to secure a progressive capitalist adaptation that distinguishes 'social democracy'.

The tendency to compromise deepened in the years after 1944. There was a loss of an organic connection between political education and agitation. The Labour Party remained the educational provider for popular groups and classes, not an educative agency of and within them. The Party lost touch with working-class interests; it failed to make socialists. Its emphasis on parliamentarianism, on a strictly constitutional politics, led to an avoidance of class struggle. In the 1940s, then, there was a distance between the Labour Party in government and the popular base which had helped bring it to power. This characteristic separation of leaders and led was inherent in the administrative and statist approach of the Labour Party.

For many people who had lived through the economic crisis of the 1930s the post-war boom was hard to understand. They had been led to expect the decline of capitalism. In the context of the new economic climate the 'people' seemed to lack revolutionary fervour, and in the face of this indifference the Labour Party became more élitist, and the professional, middle-class Fabians began to stress policy-making from the centre. Fabianism has been concerned with a mission of managing and reforming capitalist society. The Labour Party, instead of considering working-class interests as the interests of the nation as a whole, subordinated them to the interests of capital.

The main characteristic of the Labour Party's social democratic repertoire that directly shaped state policy during the 1960s was the emphasis on education as state schooling, the absence of a more direct popular educative role, and the stress on a politics of access at the expense of struggle over content, context or control.

Characteristic of the 1960s was a close alliance between Labour and particular groups of intellectuals. They included sociologists such as Douglas, Marshall, Glass, Halsey and Floud.[2] The founders of the sociology of education were never really concerned with politics of class but always with a politics of status, with equality of opportunity, more social mobility, and, beyond that, with a lessening of social divisions. They looked at homes and schools as the sites of problems and pathologies rather than at society as a whole.[3] Equality for them became less and less an end in itself and more a means to social order and cohesion, while fundamental social relations remained unmodified. The stress on social background displaced attention and blame from an unequal society. The Labour Party's orientation was towards reform through the state rather than towards popular knowledge and agitation.

Let me reiterate the authors' four main criticisms of the Labour Party's educational policy. First, the contradictoriness of Labour's repertoire. Labour attempted to serve two masters: popular interests *and* those of capital. Secondly, the absence of a direct educational relation to the working class. Labour had no direct educative connection with the popular groups and classes. Thirdly, the non-popular character of the 1960s alliance. Education became a matter of experts, and working-class people figured only as problems, the 'objects' of policy. Fourthly, the limits of a narrow, statist politics focussing exclusively on 'access'. If we take account of the above factors, the exhaustion and collapse of the social democratic repertoire in the 1970s is not difficult to understand. When the conservative offensive came and the cuts in expenditure were imposed, there was a lack of resistance on behalf of education as a social service.

In the last part of the book the authors describe how 'the disintegration of social democratic assumptions then came together with the new agenda and the weight of press polemic to allow its grateful and agile adoption by the Labour leadership.'[4] The active restructuring of the whole educational system began, the move towards an increased centralization of the actual practices of education.

The authors note that though there has been a considerable radicalization of certain intellectual strata, there has been at the same time a long-term erosion in Britain of a popular socialism.[5] The Labour Party has very few organic links to the popular constituencies which it has historically claimed to represent. The Party has no independent educational ideals or vision of its own, no conception of what it is important to understand politically in order to transform the world in a socialist direction.

One of the many things we learn from this book is that social reproduction is only secured after considerable ideological work, and is susceptible to educational work of an oppositional or counter-hegemonic kind. 'The discrediting of the old social democratic terms and the development of a new policy by the right shows how new definitions can be constructed and put to work to realize changes in state action.'[6]

The authors conclude with some theses with which I completely agree; indeed, they are also the central arguments of this book: that schooling plays a role in winning the consent necessary to run a divided society, and that it plays a part in the reproduction of labour power. They stress the point that the politics of schooling is part of a wider process of bidding for consent. Hence the importance of Gramsci's concept of hegemony and his views on the role of intellectuals — topics that will be explored in the next chapter.

Some Comments on *Unpopular Education*

Though the authors' analysis is correct and is a valuable contribution to our understanding of education, I have a few reservations. I think that one of the weaknesses of the book is that though it shows the failure of Labour Party educational policies it does not fully explain the origins of social democracy. As the book begins with a discussion of the 1944 Act little space (six pages) is given to the Labour Party and education before the war.[7] It does not discuss why social democracy has been the dominant political belief of the Labour Party, and why so many socialists after the Second World War actually believed in the validity of the notion of 'educational opportunity', of individual mobility through educational success.

Unpopular Education attempts to demonstrate the link between theory and educational policy. The authors stress the influence of *the ideas of individuals* in the formation of policy. For example:

> As an academic economist Vaizey played a part in the development of bodies of knowledge (the economics of education, development and 'modernization') that provided the basis for the practical common sense of 1960's educational policy makers.... He combined the worlds of professional economics, high university politics, and international organizations with those of social democratic politics, public inquiries and direct personal advice to leading politicians.[8]

I want to make two points about this. First, the authors' focus on education policy enables them as historians to look at the formulators of public policy; they quote from 'keytexts' to provide empirical evidence of the views of (say) Keynes, Vaizey, Crosland and others. But one of the failings of this method of looking at what people have said is that sometimes people act in ways contrary to what they say they believe. Secondly, this approach gives the impression that the history of education was made by influential individuals. According to their account 'a few selected "experts" gained privileged access to powerful personnel in the Labour Party and the state, and were thus able to influence considerably the politics of schooling from the top downwards.'[9] The authors quote from an interview with Crosland where he describes meetings in his house: 'People like John Vaizey, Michael Young, Noel Annan, Asa Briggs, David Donnison and so on had very "serious" and "very unacademic" discussions there, always around matters where a decision was required.'[10]

This quotation is an example of theoretical humanism which, as I argued in the first part of the book, neglects economic determinations whilst stressing the effectivity of individual actors. The authors stress that the crisis is a crisis in hegemony and neglect, in my view, its economic aspects. It is true that there is a section on Braverman's thesis (the historical tendency towards the deskilling of the larger part of the labour force), but I would want to argue that much greater emphasis should have been placed on the structural contradictions within capitalism.[11]

Though it is stated that the family was an important factor in the politics of the 1960s, the authors have not attempted a systematic treatment of the present-day family-school relationship. An additional weakness of the book, which they admit, is the neglect of the problem of the relationship between class, race, and gender. They constantly refer to these categories, but there is no theoretical attempt to analyze the oppression of specific groups such as women and black people, nor do they comment on the interrelationship of the three categories.

The emphasis on statist social policy has led the authors to another omission: the world of the school itself. One can't help feeling that a book on the history of education of our time should deal with more than 'education policy'. What about teachers, their class location, their experience within the schools, their teaching?

Though *Unpopular Education* contains a trenchant criticism of the model of the intellectual as academic adviser — a non-popular, statist and anti-educational form of the relationship between intellectual work and politics — it says nothing about intellectuals as such. The category is completely untheorized. In the following section, therefore, I will focus on the debate about the class position of intellectuals. First, I will discuss the class position of teachers in the social structure, their experience within the apparatus, their teaching styles and practices and, finally, the problem in formulating and applying principles of a marxist pedagogy.

The Class Position of Intellectuals

As intellectuals play key roles in the reproduction of capitalist social relations and capitalist culture, it is important to analyze their class location. By intellectuals I mean those people whose activity or function is primarily that of elaborating and disseminating ideas. It is my contention that, as teachers are involved in these activities, they are therefore intellectuals because of their function in the social formation. Only when we know the class position of teachers as intellectual labour will we be able to fully understand their role in the class struggle.

Are intellectuals part of the working class? In marxism workers are defined as those people who do not own their own means of production and thus must seek employment from capital or the state in order to live. Some marxists argue that all people who have nothing to sell but their labour power are workers. Teachers are wage-labourers, and so they are part of the working class. But other marxists contend that though wage labour is an important aspect of the social relations of production there are other aspects to be considered. Workers are not simply wage-labourers, they are wage-labourers who do not control the use of their own labour and do not control the labour of others. The extent to which teachers control the use of their own labour varies enormously according to the position of the teacher in the institution and the status of the institution within the education system. And yet teachers control the labour of their students. Most teachers are in a relationship which perpetuates paternalistic élitism and control of knowledge; it is not surprising that this produces passivity and resentment amongst working-class pupils.

Gramsci's conception of intellectuals stressed the dynamic rather than the static nature of class relations. He emphasized the specific function that they play in the class struggle.[12] In his view they tend to become polarized into two camps. Those intellectuals who contribute to the hegemony of bourgeois ideology form a part of the bourgeois class; those who combat bourgeois ideology and contribute to the counter-hegemony of the proletariat are part of the working class.

Now, two objections can be made to this view. They arise from the fact that though Gramsci stresses the *functions* of intellectuals he neglects the *structural* positions held by intellectuals. Firstly, by arguing that all intellectuals whose activity reproduces the hegemony of the bourgeoisie are part of the bourgeois class itself Gramsci tends to minimize the antagonism between many of these intellectuals and the bourgeoisie. Whilst it is true that most teachers contribute to the ideological hegemony of the bourgeoisie, it is also true that many categories of teachers are oppressed in various ways by the bourgeoisie. In other words, though many teachers may be functionally organic intellectuals of the bourgeoisie, structurally they are not members of the bourgeois class.

Secondly, it is important to distinguish between the intellectuals who have positions of control in an ideological state apparatus and those who merely work within it. The Vice-Chancellor of Oxford or Cambridge University, for example, has a position of considerable authority, but many teachers in comprehensive schools have very little autonomy.

Teachers and Social Reproduction

Nicos Poulantzas has argued that intellectuals cannot be considered part of the working class because they are generally unproductive. As there is an important debate about teachers and others involved in 'social reproduction', I will try and make the distinction between productive and unproductive labour clear. Productive labour produces surplus value for capital; unproductive labour is an expense which does not produce a value greater than itself. Many economists argue that those who are involved in social reproduction are unproductive. Mandel has correctly pointed out that education does not itself create value and that costs of education are deductions from social revenue rather than expenditure of social capital: 'While the revenue spent on education undoubtedly increases social labour capacity, indeed forms certain necessary conditions of labour, it does not itself create value. It is thus not surprising that capital will only invest in education in selected sectors and by way of exception.'[13]

To return to Poulantzas' argument; he contends that intellectuals cannot be considered part of the working class because they are generally unproductive labourers and because they do not engage in manual labour.[14] He believes that intellectuals are a segment of the petty bourgeoisie (small property owners) which he calls 'the new petty bourgeoisie'. For Poulantzas the division between mental and manual labour constitutes the basic relationship of ideological domination/subordination in capitalist society. Mental labour dominates manual labour. It follows that intellectuals must be outside the working class.

Against this view it could be said that though intellectuals such as teachers are unproductive they have, like many productive workers, little or no control over their labour process and are completely subordinated to capital or the state. Secondly, it could be argued that intellectuals are not a segment of the petty bourgeoisie which, consisting of property owners, has a much more contradictory relationship to socialism than do intellectual wage labourers.

If intellectuals are not a part of the working class, and if they are not a segment of the petty bourgeoisie, as Poulantzas contends, then should they be considered a part of a completely different class?

Barbara and John Ehrenreich have suggested the existence of a class distinct from the working class, the petty bourgeoisie and the bourgeoisie, which they call the 'Professional-Managerial Class' (PMC).[15] Most salaried intellectuals, such as teachers, are placed within this class. The Ehrenreichs believe that the Professional-Managerial Class has a distinctive function in the social division of labour, namely the function of reproducing class relations.

The authors imply that all positions within an ideological state apparatus (ISA) serve the function of reproducing the capitalist class relations since the ISA itself serves this function. But they do not consider the wide differences within a school. Some positions are involved in the control of the entire apparatus (headteachers). Others involve control over specific activities within the apparatus (heads of departments). Most teachers, however, are excluded entirely from any control over either the apparatus or any important activities within it. Though it is conceded that all teachers are involved to some extent in the function of reproducing capitalist social relations, there are gradations of position within a single apparatus.

Against the Ehrenreich thesis it could be said that the activities which the PMC performs within the capitalist division of labour serve to undermine class consciousness among the working class and, secondly, that the PMC has a technocratic vision of socialism in which it would be the dominant class.

It has been argued by Erik Olin Wright that intellectuals, instead of being seen as part of a distinctive class with its own coherence and unity (the Professional-Managerial Class), should be understood as falling within *a contradictory location* within class relations.[16] In his view most intellectual wage labour would be in a 'semi-autonomous employee' category which is a contradictory class location between the working class and the petty bourgeoisie. Semi-autonomous employees, like workers, are employed by capital or state and they do not control the apparatus of production as a whole. But unlike workers, and like the petty bourgeoisie, they do have real control over much of their own labour process. In short, intellectuals share class interests with the working class and the petty bourgeoisie, but have their own interests identical to neither. While socialism promises liberation from the domination of capital, it also implies a reduction of *individual* autonomy, because in a socialist society the labour process is controlled *collectively* by workers.

The Autonomy of Teachers

It was stated earlier that different categories of teachers have different degrees of autonomy. Three basic class positions at the ideological level are outlined by Wright: (1) in the educational system the bourgeois position would be held by senior officials (government inspectors, etc.); (2) the contradictory class location is the position of most teachers who are involved in the elaboration and dissemination of bourgeois ideology; (3) the working-class location would be held by school caretakers, canteen workers, etc. The degree of autonomy of teachers within the social relations of production varies a great deal. Certain teaching positions are much closer to the working class, other positions are closer to the petty bourgeoisie.

On the whole, teachers in primary schools have considerable autonomy. But if this is the case, why is the autonomy of primary school teachers not used to resist bourgeois ideology, to present children with 'alternative' views of organizing society? I suggest that it is largely because most teachers in 'First' schools have the following characteristics: (1) they often have a limited education. The training of infant school teachers is usually child-centred, practical and untheoretical. Indeed, it is often anti-theoretical; (2) the majority of teachers consider themselves 'middle-class'. Though they say they have little interest in politics and economics, they sometimes have assumptions and practices which support bourgeois hegemony; (3) most of the teachers are married women whose freedom of choice is limited. For many, school is a convenient occupation that 'fits in' with the necessity of servicing the family. In short, radical changes are unlikely to take place in primary schools because of the characteristics of the teachers. Coercive restrictions on these teachers are unnecessary.

Secondary school teachers generally have less autonomy than their colleagues in the primary schools. This is partly because of the pressures of an examination system which is largely controlled by the universities.[17] The teaching of an overloaded syllabus has to be completed in an intense, competitive atmosphere. That teachers in primary and secondary schools have very little autonomy (in terms of the ideological content of what they teach) compared with teachers in higher education is well known.

Let us now look at the university. Undoubtedly, the university is one of the key institutions in capitalist society, but there are conflicting views of its role. There is, firstly, the idea that the function of the university is the pursuit of knowledge for its own sake. It is said that knowledge should not simply serve power or vested interests. Against this view is the idea that higher education should be practical, utilitarian, organically related to society and its 'needs'. Though the thrust of university culture is to pacify working-class intellectuals, teachers can often utilize the contradictions within their institutions. In short, the conflicting ideas of the universities' role and the institutionalization of 'academic freedom' provide a (limited) space for a few socialist teachers in which to work and challenge bourgeois ideology.

But if the relative autonomy of teachers in higher education creates the possibility of resistance to bourgeois ideology, why doesn't the capitalist class eliminate this autonomy? One answer is that whilst the relative autonomy of intellectuals is a potential threat to the bourgeoisie, this autonomy also has a useful function. The strength of bourgeois ideology rests in part upon the claim of liberal freedoms; this claim helps to reinforce the image of an open and free society.[18]

Since the beginning of the economic crisis there has been a considerable proletarianization of many segments of teachers. Any process in which the capacity of teachers to interject their own ideas into their teaching is reduced can be thought of as a process of ideological proletarianization. The proletarianization of intellectual labour which teachers are experiencing means that they are losing control over the immediate conditions of work.[19] Course loads have been increased; the school curriculum has been redirected towards an emphasis on the 'basic skills'. Gradually, programmed learning through the use of computer technology is being introduced.

Because of these and other processes many teachers in state schools are being drawn towards the working class. Teachers at the élite universities, however, remain much closer ideologically to the petty bourgeoisie. But in spite of the proletarianization of teachers at the economic level, the decrease of autonomy within the work situation, they are still engaged in the elaboration and dissemination of bourgeois ideology. And so, at the ideological level, teachers remain in a contradictory location. In Wright's view teachers are simultaneously located between the working class and the petty bourgeoisie *and* the working class and the bourgeoisie.[20] He concludes that only when the contradictory character of class location of intellectuals is understood can we begin to grasp their contradictory role in the class struggle. In the next stage of the struggle we must begin to develop appropriate political strategies for linking various kinds of intellectuals to socialist movements.

Having briefly discussed the contradictory class position of teachers and argued that different types of teachers have different degrees of autonomy, let us now turn our attention to a more practical issue: the theory and practice of teaching. What should be the attitude of socialist teachers towards 'traditional' and 'progressive' forms of teaching? And are there any 'principles' of socialist pedagogy?

'Traditional' and 'Progressive' Teaching

What is the marxist theory and practice of teaching? Unfortunately there is no clear answer; this is one of the most underdeveloped areas within marxism. Writings on socialist pedagogy are few, and in those that do exist there is a wide range of views about the form (the mode of teaching), the content, and the possible relations between them. Should teaching, for example, be 'traditional' or 'progressive'?

There are many versions of these two teaching styles. The traditional method is usually typified as being coercive and has become associated with the banking concept .of education. Paulo Freire believes that in the banking concept of education the scope of action allowed to students extends only as far as receiving, filing and storing of deposits.[21] Banking education maintains the following attitudes and practices which mirror oppressive society as a whole:

The teacher teaches and the students are taught;
The teacher knows everything and the students know nothing;
The teacher thinks and the students are thought about;
The teacher talks and the students listen — meekly;
The teacher disciplines and the students are disciplined;
The teacher chooses and enforces his choice and the students comply;
The teacher acts and the students have the illusion of acting through the action of the teacher;
The teacher chooses the programme content and the students (who were not consulted) adapt it.
The teacher confuses the authority of knowledge with his own professional authority, which he sets in opposition to the freedom of the students.
The teacher is the subject of the learning process, while the students are mere objects.

There are still many teachers who try and carry out the above practices. I see many middle-class teachers attempting to instil a set of rules which come from outside the culture and experience of young working-class people. And so, naturally, many pupils see teachers as those that 'push them around'. But what about the kind of teaching in which marxist content is taught whilst still relying on a traditional form of teaching? In this approach it is assumed that the method is unimportant, the emphasis being on the accumulation of knowledge. I believe that on this point Freire is correct when he states that 'in the revolutionary process, the leaders cannot utilize the banking method, as an interim measure, justified on grounds of expediency with the intention of *later* behaving in a genuinely revolutionary fashion. They must be revolutionary — that is to say, dialogical — from the outset.'[22]

Reacting against traditional teaching, some teachers go to the other extreme. Let me portray two types of so-called 'progressive' teaching. There are teachers who focus on the psychological problems of their students (anxiety, etc.), instead of the deeper problems of which they are only symptoms. This type of pedagogy occurs in what has been termed in America 'the therapeutic classroom'. The 'softer' approach to instruction, in which coercion is replaced by manipulation, is merely a more opaque and deceptive method of control than traditional, banking education.

Another version of progressivism should also be noted. The underlying assumption of 'progressive teaching' is that nothing can be learned unless it has meaning and is relevant to the experience of the student. It is argued that, as knowledge is socially constructed, *the experiences of the individual* are always valuable and valid. As many teachers say, 'you start with the pupils' experience and hope to build on it.' I know many socialist teachers who adopt this approach, which is (partly) based on the presuppositions of humanist marxism. It usually stems from a fear that the teacher may be acting in a positivist/authoritarian manner and from a genuine concern to treat everyone as peers and equals.

'Progressivism' is successful to some extent as it does get pupils emotionally involved in questions of race and sex discrimination, for example. I believe, however, that many pupils remain 'experience-bound', unable to see issues in broader perspective. They see problems in too personalized and subjective a manner. In short, this approach limits the development of knowledge in children by closeting them in their own experiences without allowing them to learn *new* things unrelated to their own life style.

Moreover, this type of teaching has the characteristic feature of validating every aspect of working-class experience, but what happens when that experience includes racism, sexism, national chauvinism? There seems to be a danger in using the experiences of the pupil as the source of validity. Romanticizing some aspects of working-class experience may be detrimental to their liberation.

I suggest that we should try and understand the dichotomy between traditional and progressive teaching in terms of marxist dialectics. Traditional and progressive teaching form a contradiction.[23] In dialectical thought a contradiction connotes dynamic tension between two opposing forces, which are continually being overcome and transformed. Two important aspects should be considered: experience and persuasion. I have stressed the point that many (phenomenologists and) humanist marxists feel that students are not taught to value their own experience as a source of knowledge. The teacher should, therefore, base the work in class as much as possible on the background and experience of the students and, by skilful questioning, get them to participate in the learning process. On the other hand, though the experiences of students must be taken seriously as one dimension within the creation of radical consciousness, I would argue that *experience must be mediated through conceptual categories.*

In the type of teaching that I envisage — that transcends traditional and progressive polarities — a teacher could be persuasive without using coercion or manipulation. I would argue that neither a person's capacity for choice nor ability to act on that choice is impaired by persuasion. The aim of such teaching would be that students should emerge with an analytical approach to problems and with a comprehension of underlying forces. It is no use pretending that studying marxism is easy or painless — it requires effort, time and hard work.

Principles of Socialist Pedagogy

In a book entitled *Studies in Socialist Pedagogy* it has been asserted that educational strategy should be based on four principles, all of which are to be found in the works of Marx, Lenin, Gramsci, Mao.[24] These injunctions are: (1) the educator must be educated. One meaning of this phrase is that the teacher must collaborate with students in order to learn from them. Teachers must learn everything they can from their students about their lives and experiences; (2) as educators and socialists, our task is to help the working class achieve theoretical consciousness of what it already knows and experiences, not to tell it that it knows nothing; (3) socialist theory emphasizes a politics of active participation rather than one of passive representation. This is really the principle of self-determination; (4) the task of the socialist educator, in cooperation with students, is to advance the critical assimilation of the entire cultural heritage of world history — including the hidden heritage of oppressed and exploited groups.

Though I believe that these principles are very important for teachers' practice, I would like to comment on them as *they are not so unproblematic as they may first appear.* First, the educator must be educated; I am not sure what this phrase means. If it implies that teachers must learn from their students, one immediate problem teachers face is the bourgeois ideology of many students. As Bertell Ollman has remarked, the most troublesome notions are the students' conceptions of human nature, their view of society as the sum of separate individuals; the tendency to reduce social problems to problems of individual psychology; and their identification of marxism with Soviet and Chinese practice.[25]

The second point, concerning our task as educator being to help the working class achieve theoretical consciousness, is an important one — it raises the issue of the role of teachers/intellectuals and their relationship with the proletariat. I think what should be remembered is the distinction between the 'vanguard' and the 'élite'; in the past there has often been a tendency for the former to become the élite. The third and fourth 'injunctions' can be taken together. Let us look at the question of 'the assimilation of the entire cultural heritage'. This point is particularly associated with Lenin, who insisted that 'the teaching, training and education of the youth must proceed from the material that has been left to us by the old society. We can build communism only ... by using the stock of human forces and means that have been left to us by the old society.'[26]

Let me place Lenin's point of view in the context of his time. One of the most important issues to emerge after the Russian Revolution was the cultural revolution. Whilst everyone was at one on the importance of culture, there were controversies about its meaning, its content and function in the period of transition. The main controversy was this: As the proletariat was now the new ruling class, should it create its own class culture, its own art, its own marxist science? Or should the proletariat utilize bourgeois culture inherited from capitalism?

According to Claudin-Urondo, Lenin believed that the revolution was threatened because the masses lacked cultural knowledge.[27] 'Civilization' was associated with the western countries, with their highly developed productive forces, rationalized organization of labour, and advanced science and technology. They offered Russia a ready-made model. Scientific and technological knowledge was an achievement of advanced capitalism and all that was needed was to take it over so that the masses could 'learn' it. Lenin conceived science and technology as *neutral* entities, rather like tools, the function of which can change depending on the use being made of them. As there must be complete assimilation of scientific culture, bourgeois experts must be fully utilized.

Claudin-Urondo has described how Lenin's rejection of the concept of proletarian culture brought him in conflict with Proletkult, the organization whose aim was to create a new class culture. Proletkult maintained that bourgeois culture cannot serve the interests of the proletarian régime. Without science socialism is impossible, and it is also impossible with bourgeois science. Whilst Proletkult held that the new culture could be realized only by the proletariat itself, Lenin believed that the proletariat was incapable of building the new society without recourse to bourgeois culture and specialists. The proletariat could only develop a narrow trade-union consciousness, and as it was incapable of liberating itself, it must be elevated to knowledge. Hence the need for a vanguard, the party. The same lack of culture in the masses, which makes the party's intervention indispensable, gives rise at the same time to the necessity for the party to directly manage the state on their behalf.

The Bolsheviks took over from the Second International the notion that western societies were the only model for the building of socialist society. Lenin wished to adopt the industry of western countries, to catch up and surpass them. He argued (as did Trotsky) that there was no need to invent some original way of organizing labour, as capitalism had created and perfected one that was immediately usable. Lenin introduced the scientific management of industry (the system devised by F.W. Taylor and used by Ford) without examining its inherently alienating character. Just as the proletariat cannot acquire class consciousness by its own efforts, it cannot acquire competence in 'management'. The proletariat was therefore expected to delegate its powers to the party. This process of 'substitution', whereby the party tended to substitute itself for the class, led to the proletariat being excluded from power. Lenin did not realize that the stress on absolute subordination in production and to the party contained the danger of influencing the general character of the new society at every level. In short, Lenin's assumptions contributed to a process the consequences of which were alien to the aims of the Russian Revolution and which he would have been the first to denounce. He would certainly not have approved of the fate of his own ideas.

Many of the questions discussed in this chapter, the nature of socialist teaching, the role of teachers/intellectuals, the relationship of the party to the masses, are the concerns of Gramsci's thought. It is to a study of Gramsci's work, therefore, that we now turn.

Chapter 10

Education and Social Change: The work of Gramsci

I now turn to a deeper exploration of the main themes of the last chapter: the role of teachers, different methods of pedagogy, the function of intellectuals, and the possibilities of social change. I will do this by looking at the work of the Italian marxist Antonio Gramsci. By stressing his deep understanding of the importance of culture and thought in the development of history I return to the themes discussed at the beginning of the book. Gramsci gave considerable autonomy to the world of ideas — for him the possibility of social change largely depended on the education (in the widest sense) of the working class.

I will begin by giving an exposition of Gramsci's views on education, on the teaching of young children, and the role of the school. There is then a discussion about progressive, child-centred education. Criticisms are made of recent interpretations that convert Gramsci into a 'liberal philosopher of education' whilst ignoring his revolutionary praxis. Later sections of the chapter deal with the role of intellectuals and the struggle to create a counter-hegemony. Finally, attention is focussed on two questions: Why are there so many contradictory interpretations of Gramsci's thought? And why do so many reformists seek to adapt and recuperate his work?

It is typical of Antonio Gramsci, one of the founders of the Italian Communist Party, that when he was arrested by Mussolini's police in 1926 and sent to the island of Ustica — the beginning of nine years spent in fascist prisons — he was soon organizing classes for the other inmates. It was because Gramsci believed that political revolutions are preceded by the creation of a new cultural climate that he was always insistent on the need to educate the workers in the widest possible sense. An essential element in Gramsci's political philosophy was that the revolution, and the preparation for it, would involve a profound change in the consciousness of the masses. It is this understanding of the cultural aspect of social relations, the importance of education and its relation to politics, that makes Gramsci's contribution to marxism so outstanding.

Gramsci's ideas can only be understood in the context of the intellectual climate of Italy at the beginning of the century. The dominant influence was a neo-Hegelian philosopher, Benedetto Croce, and throughout his life Gramsci conducted a sustained 'dialogue' with him. What Gramsci learnt from Croce was a view of history that embraced all human activity — art, economics, morals, philosophy, politics. It was Croce that directed attention to the importance of culture and thought in the development of history, and to the function of intellectuals in society. He also took from Croce an antipathy to positivism and economic determinism. In short, Croce provided the framework within which Gramsci was to carry out his adaptation of marxist ideas to the circumstances of Italy in the twentieth century.[1]

In rejecting economic determinism and other mechanistic versions of marxism, Gramsci broke away from the fatalistic interpretations that were common at his time. Earlier in the book I discussed the terms 'base' and 'superstructure' and pointed out that the base, in general, refers to the economy and forces of production. As the superstructure is founded upon the base, the idea can arise that the base is temporally prior to the superstructure. It is often argued that if the superstructure is caused by the base, then it is necessary to reduce it to its material conditions. According to some marxists the economic factor becomes the most important 'cause', whilst the superstructure is a mere 'effect'. Gramsci fought vigorously against the mechanistic reductionism of vulgar marxists. He wanted more autonomy for the influence of ideas and stressed the active role of men and women in the process of history. He believed that human beings can become of their own volition a force in the dialectical process. The possibility of change, however, largely depended on the education of the working class.

The Teacher as Instructor

In his writings on education Gramsci is preoccupied with a wide range of topics: education and class, the ideology of education, curriculum reform, standards, literacy, relations between school and home, relations between school and work (vocationalism), and the comprehensive school. I propose only to outline Gramsci's views on the role of teachers, the function of schools, and different methods of pedagogy.

Gramsci always insisted upon the need for didactic, authoritative teaching and the disciplined application by the learner to academic work. There was to be rigorous, formal study of reading, writing, science, geography and history. But instruction did not necessarily turn a pupil into a passive recipient; the pupil could be actively assimilating and structuring knowledge whilst s/he was receiving instruction; indeed, 'the relationship between teacher and pupil is active and reciprocal so that every teacher is also a pupil and every pupil a teacher.'[2]

In Gramsci's view one of the main objects of schooling was the complete mastery of the common standard form of the language and a high standard of literacy:

> If it is true that every language contains the elements of a conception of the world and of a culture, it could also be true that from anyone's language one can assess the greater or lesser complexity of his conception of the world. Someone who only speaks dialect, or understands the standard language incompletely, necessarily has an intuition of the world which is more or less limited and provincial, which is fossilised and anachronistic in relation to the major currents of thought which dominate world history.[3]

As it is generally acknowledged that linguistic domination implies cultural subordination, one implication for us as teachers is quite clear: working-class children need a *mastery* of language skills.

Aware that the culture of the child's family is often discrepant with the culture transmitted by the school, Gramsci saw the child's own subculture as a bridge to the mainstream culture. In this process the teachers' role was to enforce linguistic discipline and accuracy and to transmit an understanding of mainstream culture.

Gramsci emphasized learning not only as a 'process', but also as a 'product'. Gramsci wrote of the Italian elementary school before the 1923 fascist education reform: 'Previously, the pupils at least acquired a certain "baggage" or "equipment" (according to taste) of concrete facts. Now that the teacher must be specifically a philosopher and aesthete, the pupil does not bother with concrete facts and fills his head with formulae and words which usually mean nothing to him, and which are forgotten at once.'[4] Schooling, then, was concerned with the acquisition of cognitive 'baggage' or equipment. Schooling was *work* — there could be no learning without effort, drill, even drudgery: 'Would a scholar at the age of forty be able to sit for sixteen hours on end at his work-table if he had not, as a child, compulsorily, through mechanical coercion, acquired the psycho-physical habits?'[5]

School against Folklore

Gramsci made important distinctions between common sense and good sense; popular philosophy and scientific philosophy. He held that every social stratum has its own common sense — a blend of good sense and folkloristic superstition. Common sense is a philosophy or world view which is flawed with superstition and incoherence. Good sense is a state of mind in which common sense is purged of superstition and folklore. The aim of schools is to struggle against folklore, to transform the child's common sense to good sense.

In Gramsci's view philosophy exists at all cultural levels from 'common' or 'popular' philosophy to the systematic world view of the specialist, which he called 'scientific' philosophy. In schools pupils could be moving from the level of the spontaneous, unconscious philosophy towards philosophers' philosophy: instead of thinking in a disjointed, episodic way they should begin thinking in a systematic, coherent and critical fashion.[6] Of course he realized that most children were not going to be professional philosophers, and so he stressed that the aim of the school should be the development of good sense through exposure to philosophers' philosophy.

He also pointed out that, despite the inability of common philosophy to sustain a coherent, systematic world view, 'it is not possible to separate what is known as "scientific" philosophy from "popular" philosophy. These are extremes of a spectrum rather than contradictory oppositions.' Gramsci held that, in a sense, 'everyone is a philosopher and that it is not a question of introducing from scratch a scientific form of thought into everyone's individual life, but of renovating and making "critical" an already existing activity.'[7] He therefore emphasized the need to keep in touch with the simple as a necessary condition for 'elaborating a form of thought superior to "common sense" and coherent on a scientific plane.'

But who was to have the task of elaborating a superior form of thought, the transformation of common sense to good sense? It was to be the function of intellectuals of the subordinate class to develop the rational part of common sense, to give the 'good sense' present in common sense an ideological coherence and unity. The work of intellectual élites 'cannot be formed or developed without a hierarchy of authority and intellectual competence growing up within them.'[8] But before there is a detailed consideration of intellectuals and their role in society, I must examine the reasons for Gramsci's opposition to 'progressive education.'

Progressive Education and Fascism

There was a reorganization of Italian elementary schools in 1923, a reform initiated by Giovanni Gentile, Mussolini's Minister of Public Instruction. It is an interesting irony that the reforms, though carried out by a fascist government, tended towards the 'liberalization' of education. Accounts of the principles underlying the reforms read like summaries of progressive educational theory, what we would now call 'child-centred' ideas.

Gramsci strongly attacked Gentile's reorganization of education. Why was he so opposed to these liberalizing 'reforms'? Gentile's programme, originating from idealist philosophy, was based on an inadequate analysis of society. The reforms were intended to encourage spontaneity, learning from experience, and freedom of expression. 'But as with most idealistic conceptions of education "freedom" reflected only that which was compatible with the existing social and economic order. So that where the philosophers strove towards the higher ideals of education, the structure of the education system itself denied those very ideals....'[9] Gramsci remarked that despite Gentile's efforts the Italian educational system would still only cater for an intellectual aristocracy.

Gramsci's argument against free pupil activity and spontaneity was that they leave the individual a prey to the fortuitous, chaotic and arbitrary impact of the environment. Such an abandonment of children implied the abdication of the older generation's responsibility for education. This type of schooling seems to leave pupils without the cognitive resources to question and criticize. I am inclined to believe that this is true, but the problem is that it is hard to break our way of thinking which habitually associates liberal or progressive pedagogy with a social democratic society and links teacher-directed schooling, the structured transmission of academic knowledge, with authoritarian régimes. And so the question arises: why did a fascist state enact such a liberal educational reform? Inevitably, we will have to ask further questions about the nature of progressive education: is progressive education fundamentally a neutral process which can be equally used by social democratic and fascist régimes for their own purposes?

One of the problems in the sociology of education is that we do not fully understand the relationship between consciousness and the functions of schooling. The effects of certain types of schooling cannot always be predicted. As I mentioned in chapter 5, there are some writers, like Bowles and Gintis, who argue that the organization and social relationship of schools correspond to the economic and political needs and the ideological norms of society.[10] In this correspondence model the school reflects society. It is assumed that the young are socialized into accepting the *status quo* through the disciplines and routines of the school. But, as we all know, the discipline imposed by adults is as likely to produce resistance as conformity.

One of the relationships between consciousness and functions of schooling that we should consider is the link between progressivism and fascism. It has been asserted by Harold Entwistle that a political system like fascism may be well served by an educational ideology which derides the acquisition of information and which elevates the experience of the immature above knowledge to be acquired and facts to be stored.[11] Is this in fact true? Does a child-centred progressive education leave children so immature that authoritarian leaders can take political control? If we suppose this is so, why was progressive education not taken up in Nazi Germany?

Consider the case of contemporary Britain, where the move to the Right in politics during the last few years has gone hand in hand with an assault on progressive education.[12] I have argued elsewhere that there has been a shift by the capitalist state towards greater authority and authoritarianism in schools; but this increasing emphasis does not necessarily mean that there will be an increase in 'educational' instruction and the acquisition of cognitive knowledge, so that people can question more readily the propaganda, the systematic distortion of reality that surrounds them. Entwistle's book on Gramsci expresses more than the author's belief in individualism, tradition and authority; it is an attempt to portray a revolutionary as a reformist. It is worth examining his text as a case-study of the workings of the process of incorporation. Let us see how the 'dangerous' is made 'safe'.

The Recuperation of Gramsci

Gramsci has now become a 'theorist of education'. Attempts are being made, like those of Entwistle, to assimilate Gramsci's thought into the established domain of social democratic philosophy of education. Entwistle's main purpose is to stress the contradiction between Gramsci's radical political theory and his support for traditional educational practice: 'the paradox of conservative educational theory in service of a radical political ideology.'

I believe Gramsci took his theory of education to be integral to his political theory; but by exclusively focussing on Gramsci's thesis on education Entwistle separates it from politics. This type of separation is common among academics in the field of education, one effect of such a process being that it renders schooling 'neutral'. (But whatever some people may wish, schools *cannot* be neutral.) Gramsci is thus presented as an educational theorist, a philosopher, rather than a political revolutionary with stimulating insights about education.

In writing his book Entwistle seems to have at least four aims. His first aim, in the early section of the text, is to attack the sociology of education associated with the phenomenological approach of Michael F.D. Young. He shows that the views of these radicals were not shared by Gramsci; that, in fact, Gramsci believed in all the propositions against which they have fought: the child is a deficit system, facts are to be 'banked', the teacher is an authority, knowledge is objective, hierarchical, and so forth. Thus Entwistle uses Gramsci as a stick with which to beat the sociologists. But they hardly need that type of criticism now; most of them moved on from the relativistic, phenomenological position a long time ago.[13]

The author, then, uses his subject to attack progressive, child-centred education, but I believe that it is simplistic to categorize Gramsci as a traditionalist. Entwistle makes out, for example, that Gramsci can be placed among those who believe in 'banking' knowledge. Though Gramsci does give this impression in *some* of his notes, he cannot be classified so neatly:

> We need to free ourselves from the habit of seeing culture as encyclopaedic knowledge, and human beings as mere receptacles to be stuffed full of empirical data and a mass of raw, unconnected facts, which have to be filed in the brain as in the columns of a dictionary, enabling their owner to respond to the various stimuli of the outside world. This form of culture is really dangerous, particularly for the proletariat.... [14]

Entwistle's discussion remains at a superficial level, as he only operates with two terms: spontaneity versus authority, terms which remain undefined and ambiguous. In my view this is a false opposition, implying that all the varied activities undertaken in schools can be categorized in one polarity or the other.

The attack on progressive education inevitably leads to the propagation of the virtues of traditional education and *authority*: 'When read in isolation from the rest of his work, there is no doubt that Gramsci's explicitly educational writing reads like a Black Paper forty years before its time.'[15]

Entwistle's interpretation of Gramsci's thought always stresses the necessity for 'authority', the existence of hierarchies, the need for 'experts' and, by implication, the importance of leaders. But Entwistle presents a one-sided, de-politicized view of Gramsci. In the *Prison Notebooks* Gramsci writes: 'In the formation of leaders ... is it the intention that there should always be rulers and ruled, or is it the objective to create the conditions in which this division is no longer necessary?'[16] By omitting Gramsci's question Entwistle blurs the crucial difference between theorists of the Left and the Right on these issues.

Entwistle is so keen to show that Gramsci's views represent 'a coherent socio-pedagogical theory' that he never discusses whether some of Gramsci's ideas about the teaching of young children may be limited — or wrong.

Finally, Entwistle aims to assimilate Gramsci's life-work into bourgeois education theory. The author's method is to relate Gramsci's beliefs to some establishment philosopher or right-wing educationalist, for example, Barzun, Dewey, Flew, Peters, Whitehead. Consider the effect of repetition on the reader of statements like the following:

For Gramsci, cultural creativity (as Dewey also insisted) requires that the would-be innovator takes a tradition into himself.[17]

Notwithstanding superficial appearances to the contrary, examinations do not turn the learner into 'a passive and mechanical recipient, a gramophone record'. Gramsci's position was exactly that of Flew.[18]

In common with Whitehead who was writing at much the same time, Gramsci was in no doubt about the need for a stage of precision in the learning cycle.[19]

Gramsci's notion of education as a struggle against instincts recalls R.S. Peters' notion of 'education as initiation' and his characterization of the initiation process as akin to one of bringing the barbarians inside the gates of civilization.[20]

Here Gramsci seemed to be taking a stance similar to that of Jacques Barzun who has argued there cannot be 'education without instruction, nor instruction without authority.[21]

Consider, for a moment, the assertions about tradition and 'education as initiation'. I would argue that there is no warrant in Gramsci for assuming, as Entwistle does, that it is the teacher's role or duty to transmit mainstream culture to the masses. What Gramsci stressed was that *oppositional criticism* of both the highest cultural manifestations of the past and of the dominant culture of the day are the fundamental intellectual tasks. As Philip Simpson has correctly pointed out, Gramsci did understand and value traditional mainstream culture, but as a critical opponent.[22]

Another feature that Entwistle emphasizes in Gramsci's writing is that of effort, drill and drudgery. In his portrayal of Gramsci's thought Entwistle makes this appear as an aspect of the former's conservatism, his 'traditionalist' view of education. He fails to realize that Gramsci's emphasis on work is an aspect of his understanding of Marx. Work is a fundamental category in Marx because it has a transforming power.[23] Labour is a condition of freedom in that by means of labour human beings satisfy their needs and can liberate themselves from the constraints of nature. And so it is not surprising that Gramsci stressed work as a vital principle. Nature is mastered and society changed through work. Gramsci's writings suggest that he saw education as being not only about self-discipline and self-knowledge but about the possibilities of change.

I want to argue that Gramsci's position is always much more complex than Entwistle realizes. Entwistle's misinterpretation is partly due to a lack of knowledge about Marx and marxist concepts, and because he writes about marxism from a social democratic frame of reference. My main criticism of Entwistle is that he converts Gramsci into a reformist. Let me give just three examples:

Gramsci seemed committed to the traditional conception of equality of opportunity, where the objective is the cultivation of meritocracy from amongst all the available talent.[24]

But it was the Factory Council which was concerned with political and economic education.... This underlines Gramsci's notion that counter-hegemonic activity must be educational and not simply an attempt at forcible replacement of the capitalist class.[25]

The meaning and practical implications for teachers of Gramsci's theory of praxis must be sought elsewhere — in his notion of teaching as an essentially philosophical task.[26]

Entwistle points out that Gramsci insists 'that everyone is a philosopher though in his own way and unconsciously' and that it is necessary to transform what is implicit, contradictory, and fragmentary in the masses. Again, what is revealing here is what Entwistle does not say, what he excludes. Nowhere in his book does one feel the force of Gramsci's argument that the necessity of this transformation, the purpose of this critical and systematic awareness is 'the formation of a popular collective will to action'. Thus Gramsci is made into a Fabian reformist; praxis is transformed into philosophy. This process is reflected in Entwistle's own work; in the last few pages of his book he withdraws and focusses narrowly on education, rather than expanding from education into questions of revolutionary social change. Gramsci said somewhere that in a time of crisis the traditional intellectual returns to the fold.

As there are so many interpretations of his thought, so many attempts to recuperate Gramsci, it is crucial to emphasize the fact that he did not believe that the capitalist state could be reformed.[27] Gramsci constantly asserted the imperative necessity of the revolutionary overthrow of the capitalist state.

The Purpose of Schools

Such is the greatness and originality of Gramsci's contribution to marxism that there is a temptation for contemporary writers to create out of his 'notes' a complete, integrated educational theory. It is insufficiently recognized that some of Gramsci's views on the educational system arise out of the context of his own time and place. The conditions of education in Italy in the 1920s are unlike those of Britain in the 1980s; consider the difference between rural, catholic children of Sardinia and the urban, multi-ethnic, working-class pupils of Southall.

Nevertheless, Gramsci is important for us in that he raises some crucial *questions* about education, though, at the same time, we must accept that many of them are left unanswered. Gramsci's notes about schooling are really an inconclusive interrogation about the kinds of educational change which he thought desirable and necessary. That is why so much of his writing is concerned not with existing reality but with a possible one, and why some of his notes on education appear prescriptive.

For Gramsci, then, the purpose of schools is to develop a critical ⊂ consciousness through intellectual application. He argues that the school curriculum should provide not only the basis of knowing what is, but also the means whereby such a reality may be transcended. The aim of education is that it should guide people so that they may come to know and transform the world.

In the past some social scientists held that it was through changes in education that society should be transformed. But this notion over-emphasizes the role of schools; the educational system does not possess the power to do this. Though Gramsci believes that one of the main functions of the school is the creation of working-class organic intellectuals, who will develop among the masses a critical self-consciousness, he also argues that the struggle for changes in the school must be *concurrent* with other counter-hegemonic struggles. It is time we took a detailed look at the creation of intellectuals and the meaning of hegemony.

The Creation of Intellectuals

The intellectual is the pivotal concept in Gramsci's thought. His views on this matter are different from those of Marx and Lenin. Whilst Marx seems to have thought of intellectuals as coming from the bourgeois class and Lenin believed that intellectuals came from an intermediate class (probably the petty bourgeoisie), Gramsci held that intellectuals were not a separate class. In his view both the bourgeoisie and the proletariat have their own, 'organic' intellectuals. They are the organizers of social hegemony.

Gramsci wrote of traditional and organic intellectuals. They are 'traditional' when they are tied to a class belonging to a former mode of production or to a class on the way to disappearing. What was vitally important for the working class was that intellectuals should be generated from the working class itself — these he referred to as organic intellectuals (though all intellectuals are organic to some hegemonic class). Gramsci made a distinction between people who are intellectuals because this is an inevitable feature of their existence as human beings and those who perform the specific functions of intellectuals: 'All men are intellectuals ... but not all men have in society the function of intellectuals.' He defined intellectuals as those who could exercise leadership or direction, by reference to social function. What was required was an active commitment to the creation of working-class hegemony.

Gramsci was acutely aware that in the modern state there was not only force and coercion but also persuasion and consent — the willing acceptance of the values of the rulers by the ruled. He saw clearly that the rule of one class over another does not depend on economic or physical power alone, but rather on persuading the ruled to accept the system of beliefs of the ruling class and to share their moral, cultural, social values. For a class to have hegemony, it has to be seen as having the right to rule.[28] The ruling class maintain itself by a combination of dictatorship and hegemony, which are respectively institutionalized in political state power and in civil society.[29] Though the relationship between repressive state power and the institutions of civil society is never constant, one can say that the element of consent is always present in the application of force, and the element of force is always present in the achievement of consent.

If the ruling class is successful, then this will involve the minimum use of force:

> The normal exercise of hegemony in the area which has become classical, that of the parliamentary régime, is characterized by the combination of force and consensus which vary in their balance with each other, without force exceeding consensus too much. Thus it tries to achieve *that force should appear to be supported by the agreement of the majority*, expressed by the so-called organs of opinion — newspapers and associations....[30]

According to Gramsci, a successful ruling class is one which had already established its intellectual and moral *leadership* before obtaining political power. In this process the role of the intellectuals is all-important, since the achievement and maintenance of hegemony is largely a matter of education: 'Every relationship of hegemony is necessarily a pedagogic relationship.'[31] The degree of success of such an educational process will be shown by the extent to which a new consensus, a counter-hegemony is formed.

The creation of a new hegemonic culture, however, could not be spontaneous: 'There is no organization without intellectuals, that is, without organizers and leaders, in other words, without the theoretical aspect of the theory-practice nexus being distinguished concretely by the existence of a group of people "specialized" in the conceptual and philosophical elaboration of ideas.'[32] Intellectuals remain in contact with the 'simple' and indeed find in this contact the source of the problems they set out to study and resolve. It is important to stress this. The élite is organic to a particular class, articulating its predicaments, making coherent the principles and the problems raised by the masses in their political activity. These élites of intellectuals are of 'a new type which arise directly out of the masses, but remain in contact with them to become, as it were, the whale-bone in the corset.'[33]

Gramsci particularly stressed that the intellectual, organically linked to the revolutionary class, should be *a member of a political party* which provides the leadership for that class.[34] Political parties elaborate and diffuse conceptions of the world and are the crucibles where the unification of theory and practice takes place.

The Meaning of Hegemony

In Gramsci's early work hegemony is thought of in terms of building class alliances. But in his later work (the *Prison Notebooks*) hegemony is no longer a question of a simple political alliance; it is a complete fusion of economic, political, intellectual, and moral *leadership* which will be brought about by one fundamental group, and groups allied to it, through ideology. Gramsci no longer applies the term hegemony to the strategy of the proletariat, but uses it to think of the practices of the ruling classes in general. A hegemonic class is a class that has the ability to articulate the interests of other social groups to its own by means of ideological struggle. In order to exercise leadership the class must genuinely concern itself with the interests of those social groups over which it wishes to exercise hegemony. In other words, hegemony is *constructed*, not by the domination of one class or group, but with the consent of different groups — it is the terrain on which ideological struggle takes place.

There are two principal routes by which a class can become hegemonic: that of transformism and that of expansive hegemony. Transformism involves the gradual but continuous absorption of other groups, the building up of a 'passive consensus'. In this type of hegemony the masses are integrated through a system of absorption and neutralization of their interests in such a way as to prevent them from opposing those of the hegemonic class.

Gramsci contrasted this type of hegemony through absorption by what he called successful hegemony, that is to say, expansive hegemony. This had to consist in the creation of an active, direct consensus resulting from the genuine adoption of the interests of the popular classes by the hegemonic class, which would give rise to the creation of a 'national-popular will'.

Only a fundamental class (that which occupies one of the two poles in the relations of production) can become hegemonic. It should be stressed that hegemony for Gramsci is not just a purely instrumental alliance between classes; it involves the creation of a higher synthesis so that all its elements fuse in a 'collective will' which will function as the protagonist of political action. It is through ideology that this collective will is formed.

Gramsci warns us that hegemony must not be thought of mechanistically. At different 'moments' there can be different types of hegemony. Concessions have to be made to subordinate groups; moreover, hegemony is never really fully achieved — and in some societies hegemony cannot be constituted.

In short, hegemony is about transforming the old traditions and the creation of a new 'common sense'. To win power one must begin by an appeal to 'common sense'. Politics is not about domination, but the creation of a new culture. In this process ideology is a sort of cement, binding people, motivating them politically. Gramsci stressed that ideologies are neither free-floating nor merely reflections of the dominant class. The dominant ideologies are always the product of struggle.

Reform or Revolution?

It will have been noticed that there are many contradictory interpretations of Gramsci's work. Why is this? The difficulties of interpretation arise for many reasons. Firstly, Gramsci was trying to work towards new concepts with an old vocabulary. Secondly, he was writing in prison and had to disguise his concepts to pass the fascist censor. Thirdly, after Gramsci's death his work was again censored and adapted by the Italian Communist Party leadership to justify the Party's tactics.[35]

Because of their variety as well as their fragmentary nature the *Prison Notebooks* provide texts to support many different views of Gramsci's message. Gramsci is now often presented as a theorist with a non-Leninist policy that is relevant to the advanced industrial countries, a theorist deeply concerned with the question: why has capitalism been so durable in the West?

Just as there have been attempts to incorporate Gramsci into bourgeois education theory, there are attempts to assimilate him into reformist, parliamentary politics. The argument, simplified, goes like this: Gramsci suggested that in Russia a speedy frontal attack, a war of manoeuvre, with small forces, was able to abolish the domination of the coercive Tsarist state in 1917.

> In Russia the state was everything, civil society was primordial and gelatinous; in the West, there was a proper relation between state and civil society and when the state trembled a sturdy structure of civil society was at once revealed. The state was only an outer ditch, behind which there stood a powerful system of fortresses and earthworks....[36]

In the West capitalism was older, had deeper roots in society than in the East. In the advanced industrial countries there was engineering of consent instead of coercion, hegemony rather than domination. It was civil society within capitalism, the domain of consent, that became the ultimate barrier to the victory of socialism. The strategy in the West, therefore, could not be a war of manoeuvre, but should be a war of position — a long, protracted struggle. By this type of argument, against Gramsci's intentions, conclusions have been drawn from his work that lead away from revolution towards reformism. In the hands of reformists Gramsci's speculations have become a justifying argument for emphasizing cultural struggle in an attempt to create a counter-hegemony. Reformists are also repudiating classical marxist concepts such as dictatorship of the proletariat and are trying to make political alliances with elements of the bourgeoisie and to concentrate on the parliamentary road. This is Euro-communism.

What is it in the *Notebooks* that makes it possible for a revolutionary like Gramsci to be depicted as a reformist? It could be argued that Gramsci never resolved the conflict between marxism and the historical relativity and subjectivism of Croce. Joll believes that

> The fact that he remained rooted in the Italian and the European idealist cultural tradition so that, however much he reacted against them, Vico and Hegel, Sorel and Croce were in some ways as important for him as Marx and Lenin, means that it is easier *for the non-marxist* to conduct a dialogue with Gramsci than with any other marxist writer of the twentieth century.[37]

Many non-marxists and/or those who have wanted to *revise* marxism have been attracted to Gramsci precisely because of his awareness of the interaction of marxism with other philosophies. Marxist intellectuals particularly are enthusiastic about Gramsci — but is this surprising, considering the central role intellectuals play in Gramsci's work? They often justify their narrow focus on hegemony by arguing that Gramsci stressed the importance of gradual cultural transformation — as if ideas could merely be fought by other ideas. Used in this way, the concept of hegemony has tended to imply that the power of the capitalist state rests essentially on culture and consent. This form of idealism leads to scholastic academicism; there is a tendency to overrate the role played by consciousness in both the production of ideology and the overcoming of capitalist society. Moreover, there is an underestimation of the role of the armed apparatus of repression and a neglect of praxis — the unity of theory and practice. Ironically, the problem with many structuralist theories is that they also tend to neglect problems of praxis and social change.[38] Gramsci is an antidote to this; for him theory is justified only when transmuted into action.

Chapter 11

Review

Introduction

This final chapter consists of four main sections. In the first section I summarize the arguments of the book concerning the debate between humanist marxism and structuralist marxism. In the second section I reassert the importance and usefulness of teaching structuralist methods and techniques in schools and colleges. At the same time, however, I want to make it clear that I have some criticisms of 'high' structuralism. I draw attention to the worrying features of post-structuralism, how some aspects of Foucault and Lacan, for example, are being used by the 'New Right'. The third section recapitulates the educational and political ideas of Gramsci and argues that, as class struggle takes place in language, some of the new theoretical developments should be used by the Left. There is, therefore, a discussion of the ideas of a contemporary theorist, Ernesto Laclau, whose work exemplifies a useful integration of the insights of post-structuralism and marxism. The fourth section focusses on the attempt to combine the latest developments in linguistics and post-structuralism with Gramsci's concept of hegemony.

Humanist Marxism and Structuralist Marxism

In chapter 1 I focussed on Althusser's contribution to our understanding of ideology. It was stated that ideologies are materially located and are therefore best examined in the institutions and apparatuses which elaborate them. Ideologies are not merely systems of ideas — they are practices. I then tried to show that education is not an innocent practice; that the word 'education' is itself an ideological term. It should be seen as a historical category; no 'education' exists independently of the functions which it serves or the uses to which it is put.

I have emphasized, following Althusser, that the educational apparatus is a crucial ideological instrument. It incorporates new classes and fractions of classes into cultural unity, establishes a consensus of social taste, constructs common traditions, prepares people for the dull routines of adult work. What ideology does is to support existing forms of domination; by representing sectional interests as universal it justifies existing relations of power.

The chapters on history and literature dealt with the debates about humanist marxism and structuralist marxism. In chapter 2 I took Althusser as representing the structuralist position and Thompson as representing the humanist position. It was noted that the latter stressed the role of experience and agency in history and held a subjectivist view of class. Thompson and other humanists, fearing economic reductionism, feel that the stress on the economic level may deny the autonomy of the superstructure. Moreover, theoretical humanists tend to reject abstract concepts.

Against this viewpoint I argued that marxism does not identify the real with what is experienced. The empirical world is causally connected to 'deeper' levels, the structures and processes of the real. These causal connections cannot themselves be understood through experience, because neither the underlying structures nor the connection between these structures and the empirical world are themselves experienced. The connections can only be reconstructed in knowledge. In short, the construction of highly abstract concepts (such as the mode of production, the forces and relations of production) is an essential task.

I suggested that one of the problems with theoretical humanism, with its stress on the accounts which social actors give of their experience themselves, is that the accounts may be infused with ideological elements; 'misrecognition' by the actors may be involved. Secondly, humanist marxism tends to be voluntaristic; it emphasizes that men and women make history, but neglects consideration of the fact that, to some extent, history is made under conditions which are not of their own making.

Thus humanist marxism stressed consciousness, intentionality, the projects of human beings. Structuralist marxism marked a sharp break with it. Structuralism displaces the individual. One influential tendency in structuralism sees not human beings living in and through structures, but structures living in and through human beings. Culture, then, is not so much the product of an individual's consciousness as the unconscious forms and categories through which historically definite forms of consciousness are produced. Culture is as much constituted by its conditions of existence as it constitutes them.

Discussion of the controversy between humanism and structuralism was continued in chapter 3, with literature being the main topic. I focussed on the socialist humanism of Raymond Williams whose *early* work stressed lived experience and avoided any form of abstraction. It was argued that the teaching of literature from a humanist position — with its stress on experience, the capacity of people to create their own meanings and values, its voluntarism and over-subjective approach to the social formation — would mean that students would remain without an understanding of the relationship between modes of production, ideologies and cultural artifacts.

I then turned to those (post-Althusserian) structuralists like Macherey and Eagleton who are attempting to dislocate criticism from the concerns of idealist bourgeois aesthetics. After outlining Eagleton's concepts, the basic categories which enable literary production to be explained in materialist terms, I tried to show that this method could be applied to theorize 'educational modes of production'.

It was suggested that the teaching of literature is essentially an ideological operation which attempts to heal or placate class and ideological contradictions and to reinforce class differentiation. It is within the educational apparatus that the ideological function of literature — its function in reproducing the conditions and social relations of the capitalist mode of production — is most apparent.

Throughout these chapters I have tried to present both sides of the argument. In my criticism of structuralist marxists I said that they often return to the analysis of society in terms of 'systems' and 'structures', but in this move they reconstitute some of the fundamental positions of a discredited structural-functionalism. Structuralists tend to stress domination and constraint, the power of the dominant ideology; the emphasis is always on the integrative, functionalist, adaptive, *deterministic* features. According to humanist marxism, structuralist marxists neglect the role of experience and human agency; they evade the dialectic between agency and conditions. Moreover, they understate the existence of, and the possibilities for, struggle and resistance. It is not surprising, given the anti-humanist severity of structuralist marxism, that tendencies arise which reassert the individualistic, the romantic and the subjective. I would want to argue that there are aspects of human experience —

love, the brevity and frailty of human existence, the fear of one's own death and sorrow at the death of others — that cannot be easily fitted into a formal social theory. And yet these are elements of experience that marxism cannot afford to ignore.

Nevertheless, in spite of all these shortcomings, I still believe that structuralist marxism as a mode of thought should be better understood. I know that structuralism is harder to grasp than humanism, and like many other people I find it difficult to speak, to think, in structuralist terms. This is partly because humanism has become 'natural', the taken-for-granted way of looking at the world. I believe that an understanding of these controversies is crucial to what and how we teach, and that teaching would be much improved if students and teachers were systematically introduced to those debates and to the study of structuralism.

Students would have a greater appreciation of the school curriculum if they were introduced to the categories of a materialist viewpoint and given an understanding of the interrelationship between modes of production, various forms of ideology, literary, historical and other texts. I have also suggested that materialist categories should be developed capable of analyzing the (constantly changing) ways in which schools and colleges contribute to the reproduction of the conditions and relations necessary to the capitalist mode of production.

Though I have deliberately polarized the debate between humanist marxism and structuralist marxism, it is obvious that these diverse approaches are not mutually antagonistic. I suggest that we should seek a critical balance between them. Indeed, many teachers are now beginning to seek a transcendence, a supersession of these two traditions. In this task teachers can help students realize that the contradictions people confront are not natural but historically generated. In the teaching of the school curriculum we need to develop a sense of purpose and an ability to conceive of a future built on different principles than the present.

Structuralism and Post-Structuralism

Structuralism and Its Use in Schools

After discussing the polemic between humanist marxism and structuralist marxism, it was felt that we should look more deeply into the different meanings of 'structuralism' and so we began examining the concept in chapter 4. It was defined as the attempt to think everything through again in terms of language; to look at the recurrent units of repetition and attempt to isolate the governing logic; to study a 'text' as a system of signs. I gave an outline of the work of three important structuralists: Lévi-Strauss in anthropology, Barthes in semiology, and Lacan in psychoanalysis. Their ideas have influenced many contemporary marxists, ideas such as the concept of 'decentring' (the dispersal of any central unity or 'essence'), the notion of heterogeneity of discourses, and the autonomy of different practices.

I tried to show the pertinence of structuralism in two specific areas within cultural studies: how it can contribute to a new critical approach in the teaching of literature and, through an analysis of working-class youth culture, help teachers' understandings of their pupils and the society they live in. Adoption of a structuralist approach in schools would mean a radical change from current practice: there would be a shift from the view that stresses the private experience of the author, the mysterious genius, to art as production, the notion of the artist as worker transforming a given raw material.[1] But my argument is about more than the teaching of literature or cultural studies. I want to suggest that the school curriculum should be analyzed as a meaningful text using some of the insights of structuralism and semiology.

This work could take many of the paths discussed in the book. There is, for example, the tradition that has extended the structuralist and semiological analysis of myth, developed by Lévi-Strauss, into the study of culture. The texts of a culture are seen in the same way as myths, as formal attempts to resolve social contradictions in the imagination. Analyses of school knowledge as 'myth' could be most enlightening.

So much of school knowledge is produced as a commodified and closed text that I find Barthes' idea of readerly (closed) and writerly (open) texts an interesting one. I would invite students to participate in the production of knowledge by emphasizing those methods of working that open the text to interpretation. The formalist technique of defamiliarization, for example, may also be helpful. Another method that could be taught is deconstruction.

In becoming familiar with interrogative texts, deconstruction, symptomatic reading and other practices, I would hope that students would begin to regard school texts not as consumers but producers; that is to say, the emphasis would be on the role of the audience or reader in the constitution of meaning and pleasure.

One of the aims of socialist teachers should be to counter the reification of knowledge as a solid object. We need to produce school knowledge as an open text, thus inviting participation from our students. Secondly, we must aim to get students to the stage where they ask: who controls the production of meaning? In this process students could learn that reality is alterable and develop the capacity to control the apparatus of meaning production themselves.

Structuralism is useful in analyzing many aspects of culture. I focussed on working-class subcultures and said that the tensions, the conflict between those in power and those that are oppressed and exploited, can be found reflected in subculture. It was argued that subcultures are produced in response to specific historical conditions. If a style is to become genuinely popular, it must anticipate or encapsulate a mood, a moment. Teachers, it was suggested, should study youth styles because they are expressions of popular culture, manifestations of social contradictions.

Some Criticisms of 'High' Structuralism

The ideas of the extra-linguistic structuralists have had an extraordinary influence on many marxist theorists, and, though I have argued that many of the techniques can and should be used in schools, it must be conceded that structuralism as a theoretical approach has many defects. It is well-known that Sartre and many others repudiated structuralism as an objectivist philosophy which downgrades human activity and its power to transform reality. But rather than present criticisms that derive from a phenomenological point of view, I will make some comments from a marxist perspective.

The first criticism concerns the rejection of the individual in structuralism. The Italian marxist Sebastiano Timpanaro has convincingly argued that while all sciences, both the human and the natural, require that scientific explanation go beyond the mere recognition of the singularity of an object or an event, not all sciences demand the same degree of particularization.[2] This diversity stems from the nature of the objects under examination and from the aims of the research. A physician attending an individual patient would have a more particular interest than, say, a physicist for the purpose of an exact knowledge of that clinical case and its cure. The uncritical adoption of linguistics as the model for other human sciences, which must objectively be more concerned with the particular (because they deal with more complex facts in which human beings' conscious activity has a greater role), can lead to mistaken or deceptive results.

In other words, structuralists have failed to realize that in nature as well as in human institutions there exist quite different degrees of cohesion and interdependence of the individual elements:

> There are aggregates and systems, mixtures and compounds, very tight interconnections and slack or practically non-existent interconnections. To opt on *a priori* basis in every case in favour of a maximum of organicity and systematicity, and to dismiss on *a priori* basis every so-called 'atomistic' interpretation, leads inevitably to strained and arbitrary arguments.[3]

It is often suggested in anthologies on structuralism that Marx was a precursor of the movement.[4] This is only partly true. Marx believed that no science was possible without abstraction and generalization, but he made abstractions in order to return to the concrete — a fact which does not preclude the relative autonomy of abstractions. Marx was not searching for abstract models independent of experience and applicable to the 'human spirit' in general. Rather, he was looking for an abstract model which would help him to understand that transient socio-historical formation which is capitalism.

Now, structuralism is based on a philosophical position which contends that there exists the possibility of genuine knowledge independent of experience; in other words, the belief that the general nature of the world can be established by wholly non-empirical reasoning. Besides its formalism and rationalism, structuralism also emphasizes abstraction. It is obsessed with epistemological issues, with problems concerning theories of knowledge, the nature of the 'real' and so forth.

Furthermore, it could be said that structuralists emphasize impersonal rules to such an extent that they deny creativity. There is, then, in structuralism a preoccupation with formal elements and structures at the expense of content and subject matter. Moreover, there is a rejection of the individual.[5] But if structuralism abolishes the subject, how can it still claim to be objective — surely for knowledge to be known there has to be a human subject? Structuralism, in short, can be charged with emphasizing language not thought, form not content.

Structuralism and Historical Change

It is also often said that structuralism is necessarily synchronic; that it studies structures under artificial and ahistorical conditions, neglecting the systems or structures out of which they have emerged. Does structuralism neglect historical change? Lévi-Strauss and Lacan, for example, are universalists; both are concerned with the operations performed by the human mind in general, not just with the workings of particular minds at particular times.

I believe that Lévi-Strauss' analysis of myth may be a form of psychological reductionism, as what seems to determine the logic of myth, in the end, is the psychological structure of the mind, common to all people. Whilst Freud emphasized the body and its drives, for Lévi-Strauss there is only the mind, and this mind is treated as if it were a computer, a logic machine. Culture is reduced to the operation of the mind, to the physiology of the brain. On the other hand, Lévi-Strauss owes a lot to Freud (particularly to *Totem and Taboo* and *The Interpretation of Dreams*). There is such a clear parallel between the approaches of Freud and Lévi-Strauss that it has been said that the latter's structuralism is just a hygienically delibidinized version of Freudianism.[6]

Many other criticisms can be made of Lévi-Strauss' work. I have already remarked on his tendency towards universalization. His objective seems to be not the formulation of laws capable of 'grasping reality' but rather the formulation of eternal principles. Lévi-Strauss' concept of the human mind (*esprit*) is such an example. Timpanaro puts the case most succinctly: 'What is the point of exalting structuralism as a reaction against Bergonism and subjective idealism, if this reaction only leads to an objective idealism which is laden with romantic-existentialist overtones?'[7]

Furthermore, the homage paid by Lévi-Strauss to Marx as a theoretician of socio-economic relations disguises beneath its diplomatic forma an essential anti-marxism. This is the case both because 'Lévi-Strauss lacks all interest in the superstructures *qua superstructures of socio-economic structures*, and because Lévi-Strauss's spiritualistic metaphysics and anti-historicity are irreconcilable with an historical-materialist position.'[8]

It seems to me that as the synchronic assumes the major explanatory role in structuralism, historical change is neglected. It is true that Marx identified a level in which human beings are unaware of the real forces of history, yet he strongly argued against those who forget that human beings may change circumstances through revolutionary practice.

Beyond Deconstruction

So far it has been argued that many structuralists have tended to be ahistorical in their approach, divorcing their work from political considerations and consequences. Structuralism, by suppressing history, failed to challenge liberal humanism. But does post-structuralism — I am thinking particularly of Derrida and deconstruction — represent a theoretical advance?

It will be remembered that in the discourse of 'high' structuralism there is a stress on the signifier; the referent (the real thing) is bracketed out and the signified is preserved. But in post-structuralism (a tendency that developed after the events of 1968), not only does the referent vanish but also the relatively stable signified. Words no longer have real, stable meanings. The signified is seen as 'terroristic'. For post-structuralists there is only the ceaseless production of new, ever-changing meanings. There is only indeterminancy. All explanations are partial.

An analogy could be drawn between these theoretical developments and the political situation in France. In the period of 'high' structuralism there was a marxist party with a coherent policy although it was severed from any mass movement. But at the moment of post-structuralism there was a deep political disillusionment with the party. The sense of totality disappeared; all was fragmentation, everything was undecidable.

One of the consequences of deconstruction is that its emphasis on undecidability of meaning leads to a depoliticizing relativism. And so we are faced with the problem: can deconstruction, as suggested in chapter 5, be pushed towards the Left? Or are the consequences of deconstruction so serious that we must break with it and, perhaps, adopt a more social and socialist approach?

I want to suggest that the work of the Russian theorist Mikhail Bakhtin is valuable in pointing one way forward. Bakhtin, a pioneer of the marxist theory of language and literature, often published under the names of his associates, V.N. Vološinov and P.N. Medvedev. It is important to note that his best-known book *Marxism and the Philosophy of Language* is published under the name Vološinov.[9] Deeply influenced by the new school of linguistics, Bakhtin (Vološinov) was a fierce critic of Saussure's stress on *langue*. It will be remembered that for Saussure all that matters is the relationship of one sign to another within the closed system of *langue*; the question of their referent is entirely excluded. This means that there is no way in which the structure of *langue* can be explained with reference to determinations which lie outside it. What interests Bakhtin, however, is not the abstract grammar but rather the uses to which the rules comprising grammar are put in concrete social situations.

Bakhtin argued that in systematizing the rules comprising *langue* Saussure tended to smooth out the discrepancies of meaning which may be attached to the same words by virtue of the different uses to which they are put in different, socially produced linguistic practices. The proper object of linguistics should not be the fixed system of *langue* but the ways in which the rules comprising it are used, modified and adapted in concrete utterances, the determinations of which are exclusively social.

One must take account of the fact that in concrete utterances the word is inherently 'dialogical'. The word is orientated to, and takes account of the use of, words in the utterances to which it is a response. The word, ever-responsive to the words of others, is subject to incessant modification. The word is never spoken without immediately altering or qualifying discourse in the light of the possible reactions to some real (another character) or imaginary (the reader) interlocutor. Bakhtin believed that these dialogical relationships must be placed at the centre of analysis if the mechanisms whereby meaning is produced within language are to be properly understood.

In short, Bakhtin insisted on the importance of actual utterances, not just the language system, and he conceived of the sign as multi-accentuated, by which he meant that it is open to different meanings when seen from different class positions. In his theory linguistic meaning is negotiated through class-based social interaction, and it reflects and refracts an underlying material reality — that of socio-economic relations. Bakhtin sees the use of the word as part of a primarily class-based struggle for the terms in which reality is to be signified. Language, far from being a neutral horizon of fixed and given meanings, becomes an arena of class struggle as words are mobilized and fought for by different social philosophies.

I believe that Bakhtin is helpful because he has a sophisticated theory that suggests that things can be fully understood only if placed in the context of the economic, social and political relationships in which they are produced. Secondly, his theory can be integrated with the latest developments which emphasize that the process of language is a continual possibility of shift and change. Meanings have always to be constituted, and because of this there is a perpetual battle about the character of the sign and the systems which we bring to production and interpretation.[10]

The Political Effects of Lacanian Theory

In chapter 6 I said that Lacan's influence on recent French thought would be difficult to overestimate. The richness and ambiguity of his work make it possible for diverse theoretical and political currents to discover a reflection of their own preoccupations. I will briefly mention four areas where his work has had political effects.

1 Lacan influenced Althusser's theory of ideology. As I explained in chapter 1, Althusser puts forward the view that all ideology 'interpellates', hails the individual as a subject; that is to say, addresses the individual in such a way as to give him or her to understand that s/he is an autonomous agent rather than a product of a definite society limited by a definite class position. The success of this ideological mechanism can be explained in Freudian-Lacanian terms by the narcissistic fascination of the individual by an ego-ideal. Ideology flatters our belief in ourselves as autonomous subjects and distracts us from focussing on the structural determinants of our activity.
2 Some feminists have used Lacan's ideas in analyzing patriarchy. The Lacanian interpretation of Freud appeals to many women's groups, and some sections of the feminist movement have adopted the idea of cultural revolution separate from the social revolution as a necessary condition for the overthrow of patriarchy.
3 In Britain Lacan's work may be having a de-politicizing effect. This is because there is a tendency in Lacan's work to disregard realities outside of language and assume that 'discourse' is sufficient unto itself.
4 In France some of Lacan's ambiguous ideas are being utilized by the reactionary 'New Philosophers'.

Let us examine first the issue of language and then the ambiguity of Lacan's work.

What happens in the work of some contemporary theorists is that language is made (in effect) the only reality, or that reality is made a function of language. For example, post-Althusserians, such as Barry Hindess and Paul Hirst, have argued that the validity of a discourse is a matter entirely internal to that discourse itself. Since the objects of discourse exist only in and through discourse and not in any extra-discursive realm, it also follows that there can be no communication across discourses.

Drawing on the above argument, some theorists argue that art, for example, is not a mirror to reality, but a construct, produced through a particular type of language use, particular conventions or rules of construction, particular 'signifying practices'. They say that all we ever succeed in doing is comparing the terms of one discourse with those of another. Ultimately, reality is nothing more nor less than the signifying practice itself.

There are, then, theorists on the Left who seem to be stating that society is nothing but its languages and signifying practices. In many recent developments there is a

> danger of conflating the social structure of reality with its signification, by virtue of the fact that social processes and relations have to be mediated through language, and the evidence that the mediating power of language reflects back on the social process. But to say that language has a determining effect on society is a different matter from saying that society is nothing but its languages and signifying practices.[11]

In other words, what is missing in this argument is the essential distinction between meaning and reference. Though the concept of a dog cannot bark, and the concept of a woman cannot sing, nevertheless, in both cases the concept does refer to something in the real world which does do these things.[12] Although we can only talk about or represent these real things within some signifying practice or another, what is said within those practices depends for its validity not on the signifying practice alone, but on properties and qualities of the things referred to or represented. In short, I want to argue that the real world cannot be reduced to language, or to theory, but is independent of both and yet knowable.

I mentioned just now the ambiguity of Lacan's work. Though he is often depicted as the founder of 'structuralist' psychoanalysis because of the ideas borrowed from Saussure and Lévi-Strauss, his work is also a *critique* of them. Throughout the period of 'high' structuralism, with its abolition of the human agent, Lacan persisted in theorizing the place of the subject in psychoanalysis. When the structuralist orthodoxy broke down, Lacan was at the centre of the attempt to construct a notion of the subject.

In Lacan's work there is a structuralist emphasis on the determining effect of symbolic systems and yet, at the same time, there is always something which eludes and displaces such systems — the movement of the subject caught up in desire. There is, then, a profound ambiguity in Lacan's work; he is midway between the seekers of immutable structures and the celebrants of desire.

The Post-Structuralism of Foucault

After describing the structuring of subjectivity, I turned to an examination of the work of Foucault. I underlined Foucault's concern about the growth of discipline, changes in the modalities of control, and relations between knowledge and power. It is useful to note the striking similarities of Foucault's work with the central concerns of Max Weber: the role of the bureaucrat governed by the spirit of 'formalistic impersonality'; the growth of 'instrumental rationality' and systematic, strict discipline; the processes of rationalization and its consequence: the 'disenchantment of the West'.

My presentation of Foucault's work in chapter 7 was consciously ambivalent; on the one hand I emphasized the importance of his contribution to social science, but on the other hand I argued that the Foucaldian conception of politics and power is inadequate. It lacks a serious consideration of determining conditions and factors.

I think Foucault is quite wrong about the seizure of state power. But perhaps his generalizations refer to the industrial nations of western Europe rather than the developing countries. There is no doubt that it is possible to attack and seize the state. In 1979, for example, the long-lived Somoza dicatorship in Nicaragua fell before a mass insurrection led by the Sandinist movement.

Secondly, Foucault is wrong when he suggests that power in capitalism is so diffused throughout civil society that the state ceases to have any specific and privileged role as a locus of power. It is my contention that capital has a growing need for the state to facilitate capitalist planning, to assume liabilities, to conduct and contain class conflict. I would want to argue that the armed power of capital usually remains in the background and that class domination usually appears in the guise of the autonomous and neutral 'state'. When, for example, violent confrontations break out outside the factory gates, they are not directly between capital and labour; it is not capital itself but the state that conducts the conflict. It could be said that the state represents the 'coercive "moment" of capitalist class domination embodied in the most specialized, exclusive, and centralized monopoly of social force.'[13]

Against Foucault's rejection of the concept of class I want to assert that class must be defined with reference to the position of its members in the economic structure. A person's class is established by the person's objective place in the network of ownership relations, however difficult it may be to identify such places neatly. According to the structural definition of class, a person's consciousness, culture and politics do not enter the definition of the class position. As Gerry Cohen has pointed out, these exclusions are required to protect the substantive character of the marxian thesis that class position strongly conditions consciousness, culture and politics.[14] Of course, this does not mean that production relations mechanically determine class consciousness. There is a connection between production relations on the one hand and consciousness, politics and culture on the other, but it is not a simple one. There is a logic, but we cannot predicate a law about it.

The Shift to the 'New Right'

I argued that, as Foucault rejects essential marxist concepts such as ideology, state, class, and party, his work should be seen as subversive of marxism. There is no doubt that the ambiguities in Lacan and the Weberian-Nietzschean features of Foucault have infused directly into the *Nouvelle Philosophie* with its deep pessimism and its acquiescence in the *status quo*. The 'New Philosophers', a group of reactionary thinkers which includes André Glucksman and Bernard-Henry Lévy, have openly repudiated marxism and taken up some of the ideas of Lacan and Foucault.[15]

Among the main beliefs of the 'New Philosophers' are the following: that marxism is in some way responsible for the terror of the Soviet camps; that the state is the central source of social and political oppression and that therefore any politics directed towards the seizure of state power is dangerous and vain; that science always operates within, and reinforces, relations of power; that reason is inherently totalitarian. The 'New Philosophers', in short, have a vision in which conflict is no longer a political conflict between social classes, but an ethical struggle within the individual between 'the desire for submission' and 'the love of freedom'. They are saying that, in a sense, we are all oppressors and we are all oppressed.

These views are expressed clearly in Bernard-Henri Lévy's *La Barbarie à Visage humain*.[16] Lévy attacks the marxist theory in which power is seen as maintained by varying combinations of ideological mystification and naked repression. He argues that this view in which power is seen as the possession of a dominant class is wrong. Against this model Lévy deploys a vulgarized fusion of ideas drawn from Foucault and Lacan in which power becomes 'everything' and 'nothing'. It is nothing since it cannot be located in specific mechanisms of institutions; rather than being imposed from above, it filters up from below, permeating every social relation. We are the victims of the policeman in our heads, of our own exteriorization of the law.

For Lévy the most apt metaphor for power is the Freudian concept of the phantasm. Like the phantasm, power is in some sense unreal, and yet it is inescapable in its effects, it is everywhere and everything. Now, in Foucault there are at least 'resistances' counterposed to power, and in Lacan there is a subversion by the subject. But with the 'New Philosophers' there is only the impossibility of liberation.[17]

I think we should be more aware of the danger that new theories can be appropriated in a reactionary way. If the political views of the 'New Philosophers' are an outcome of the theories of Lacan and Foucault, it is perhaps time we began to question the widespread assumption on the Left that there is a spontaneous affinity between 'theoretical radicalism' and socialist politics. A full recognition of the latter makes one aware of the necessity for liberation. An important element in this is the class struggle that occurs in and over education.

Education: Teachers and Social Change

At the beginning of chapter 9 it was argued that teachers are intellectuals because of their function of disseminating ideas, and that it is important to know their class position. We may then be able to understand the role of teachers/intellectuals in the class struggle. The discussion centred on the question whether intellectuals were part of the working class, the bourgeoisie, the petty bourgeoisie, or a part of a completely different class, 'the Professional-Managerial Class'. I supported the view that intellectuals have, at present, a contradictory class location.

I then focussed on the question of teachers' autonomy. Though teachers in primary schools have considerable autonomy, radical change is unlikely to take place there. The characteristics of many primary teachers are such that the imposition of constraints by the state is unnecessary. Teachers in secondary schools have less autonomy because they are constrained by the examination system. It is in higher education that teachers have most autonomy (in terms of content). Conflicting ideas of the universities' role and institutionalization of academic freedom have provided a 'space' for socialist teachers — but this is now rapidly disappearing. In spite of the proletarianization of teachers at the economic level and the general decrease of autonomy within the work situation, teachers are nevertheless engaged in the social reproduction of capitalist relations. And so, at the ideological level, teachers remain in a contradictory location.

Having discussed teachers' class position, I turned to the question of socialist pedagogy. After outlining Freire's criticisms of 'banking education' I wrote that some teachers, reacting against traditional methods, often go to the other extreme and focus either on the 'psychological' problems, or on the 'lived experience' of their students. I suggested that we should understand the dichotomy between 'traditional' and 'progressive' teaching in terms of marxist dialectics. Some (possible) socialist educational principles were then stated and I tried to show that the application of these principles (even when agreed upon) is still difficult and problematic.

I then turned in chapter 10 to a discussion of the educational principles of Antonio Gramsci, his views on the aims of the school, the role of the teacher, and his arguments against 'progressive' education. I said that attempts were being made to assimilate Gramsci's educational thought into liberal/social democratic 'philosophy of education', and separate it from his politics.

Many reformist writers are using Gramsci's work to justify gradual, cultural change. They are interpreting the concept of hegemony in a way that implies that the power of the capitalist state rests essentially on culture and consent. In my view this interpretation of hegemony is a form of idealism; it leads to an underestimation of the role of the armed apparatus of repression and a neglect of praxis. Against so many attempts to recuperate Gramsci it is important to emphasize the fact that he was not a reformist but a revolutionary.

Gramsci particularly stressed that the intellectual, organically linked to the working class, should be a member of a political party which provides the leadership for that class. He believed that one of the main functions of the school is *the creation of working-class intellectuals* whose task it is to develop a critical self-consciousness among the masses. Following Gramsci, I have emphasized the role and function of organic intellectuals. For those becoming organic working-class intellectuals Gramsci designated two tasks: to challenge bourgeois ideologies and to foster 'popular' education. The struggle for changes in the school must be concurrent with other counter-hegemonic struggles.

The Struggle for Hegemony

Some readers will be asking themselves why I have stressed the work of Gramsci (usually typified as a humanist marxist) when I was earlier emphasizing a structuralist perspective. I believe that most commentators have stressed the differences between Gramsci and a structuralist marxist like Althusser. This is not difficult to do, but the similarities are often overlooked.

It is now generally agreed, even among his adherents, that some aspects of Althusser's early work were formalist, functionalist and theoreticist in character. Gradually, as an understanding of these shortcomings came about, Gramsci's work began to gain a new importance. Gramsci, besides repudiating any form of reductionism, emphasized the practical, social role ideologies have in organizing and mobilizing the masses. He stressed the complex role of class alliances in the creation of working-class hegemony. In many ways Gramsci's thought corrects the ahistorical, abstract and theoreticist level at which structuralist theories tend to operate.

On the other hand, some theorists like Chantal Mouffe have argued that Gramsci's ideas anticipated Althusser's problematic in several respects: the material nature of ideology, its existence as a necessary level of all social formations, and its function as the producer of subjects.[18] She finds implicit in Gramsci's work the idea that subjects are not given but are always produced by ideology so that subjectivity is always the product of social practice. This implies that ideology has a material existence. Ideology organizes action. In other words, Gramsci posits consciousness as the effect of the system of ideological relations into which the individual is inserted. Thus it is ideology which creates subjects and makes them act.

Though the tools of linguistics and psychoanalysis were not available to Gramsci, he tried to say some new things and to develop a new, non-authoritarian concept of politics and stressed the point that the process of transformation cannot come from the top downwards. Intellectuals must put their skill and knowledge at the service of the working class and help to articulate its demands.

A contemporary theorist who has combined Gramsci's notion of hegemony with the latest theoretical developments in linguistics and discourse theory is Ernesto Laclau.[19] He is highly critical of the mechanistic determinism associated with the Second International, and all forms of economism and class reductionism. At one time it was assumed by many marxists that there was a one-to-one correspondence between social classes and ideologies. Whole classes were ascribed fixed ideologies. Against this view it was argued by Poulant-zas and others that classes do not carry their world views around like number plates on their back. They do not have fixed, ascribed or unitary world views. Moreover, there is no simple alignment between the economic, the political and the ideological in the constitution of classes. Some theorists like Laclau adopt this position.

But other theorists have taken this approach to its extreme limit. Hindess and Hirst, for example, argue that discourses cannot be explained by or reduced to classes, defined exclusively at the level of the economic. Laclau's position, then, is distinct from that adopted by Hindess and Hirst, who have deconstructed classical marxism and believe that, as society does not have a unity, there are no necessary logical relationships.[20] Whilst Hindess and Hirst do not use the concept hegemony, for Laclau it is crucial. He believes that we are always in a process of hegemonic struggle and is therefore very concerned about how ideologies 'work', about their effects, and how they can be used by the Left.

Laclau agrees with Gramsci's remarks that the working class in the West has not yet taken over the state and transformed it because it has not yet created a hegemony. In contrast with the East where there was a quick 'war of manoeuvre' (the Russian Revolution of 1917), in the West, because of different conditions, there must be a long 'war of position'.[21] Laclau argues that for Gramsci the creation of a new hegemony does not consist in making a clean sweep of the existing world view and in replacing it with a completely new and already formulated one. Rather, it consists in a process of transformation of existing ideological elements. The objective of ideological struggle is not to reject the system, but to break it down to its basic elements and then to sift them through to see which ones, with some changes of content, can serve the new situation.

A successful hegemony is one which manages to create a 'collective national-popular will', and for this to happen the dominant class must be capable of articulating to its hegemonic principle all the national-popular ideological elements, since it is only if this happens that the class appears as a representative of the general interest. Gramsci's concept of ideology, then, is a practice which transforms the class character of ideological elements by their articulation to a hegemonic principle differing from the one to which they are at present articulated. This assumes that these elements do not in themselves express class interests, but that their class character is conferred upon them by the discourse to which they are articulated and by the type of subject thus created.[22]

Towards New Forms of Political Struggle

Gramsci understood that state power was not limited to the power of a single class. Political struggle does not only take place between the two fundamental antagonistic classes, since the 'political subjects' are not social classes but 'collective wills' which are comprised of an ensemble of social groups fused around a fundamental class. These groups will provide the 'historical base' of a dominant class, and it is on this terrain that the struggle for hegemony — by means of which a fundamental class tries to win over the other social groups — takes place.

Laclau argues that ideologies are transformed through the class struggle, which is carried out through the production of subjects and the articulation/disarticulation of discourses.[23] There is a struggle in ideology to disarticulate and rearticulate the structure of particular discourses. The ideological work of disarticulation refers to the way in which discourses can convert opposition and contradiction into mere difference, thereby neutralizing a potential antagonism.[24] Let's consider a concrete example, the concept of democracy. This has bourgeois class elements in that it contains notions of private property, parliamentary democracy and so forth. The working class should be able to disarticulate the bourgeois elements from 'democracy' and win the concept for itself. Socialists should absorb 'popular' and 'national' discourses, they should use these ideologies and articulate the demands of new 'subjects'.

In short, the argument is that politics arises in the articulation of relations between discourses. The politics of a discourse arises in the way it articulates and silences relations between subjects. And as there are new subjects such as women, black people and others who are against capitalism but are not classes, there should be new forms of political struggle. It is vital for the working class not to isolate itself within a ghetto of proletarian purism. On the contrary, it must try to become a 'national class' representing the interests of the increasingly numerous social groups.[25]

In summary, I have argued for a coming together of some marxist and structuralist positions and tried to relate them to education and social change. As I have shown in this chapter, I am critical of many aspects of both structuralism and post-structuralism. I have argued that some forms of structuralism are so local and technical, so little concerned with the wider social and historical issues that they are of little value to marxism. There are also some currents within post-structuralism that are actually incompatible with, and subversive of, marxism. If the problem with structuralism is its ahistorical universalism, then the problem with post-structuralism is its relativism.

Nevertheless, I believe that some of the insights and methods that derive from structuralism and post-structuralism are compatible with marxism and should be used in ideological struggle by the Left. Now, some people may think that my suggestion that socialist teachers should use some of the methods and insights of structuralism and post-structuralism in schools — whilst rejecting the perspectives as a whole — is an example of eclectic opportunism. But my defence is this: it is painfully difficult to work out whether the assumptions and arguments of current tendencies are compatible or incompatible with marxism. There is often the temptation to assume that because something is 'new' it is better or has a greater access to truth. But I am also aware that there are no simple criteria whereby theoretical developments can be checked for their acceptability or unacceptability. I believe that a multiplicity of strategies is possible in which fractions of discourse can play differing roles. Whilst I realize that persistent attempts are being made to recuperate marxist theories, to make them compatible or even congruent with the dominant social democratic paradigm, I am also acutely aware that unless the new theoretical developments are used to assist the construction of a socialist consciousness they will be used to subvert it.

Instead of the narrow structuralist displacement of history, what is needed is a form of analysis that is at once structural and historical, work which provides a rigorous study of cultural and educational forms in the context of historical and economic processes.

I have made it clear that I am sympathetic to some current attempts to combine post-structuralist insights with the marxist concept of hegemony. I mentioned the work of Ernesto Laclau and Chantal Mouffe as examples of the attempt to integrate post-structuralist treatments of discourse with a neo-Gramscian non-reductionist politics. According to this view, the main issue is that of constructing popular alliances out of the multiplicity of subjects (class, race, gender, family, nation, etc.) that are currently relevant. Of course, alliances can only function effectively when they relate to the spontaneous projects and experiences of people involved in their own struggles.

Though there is a danger that Laclau's type of discourse analysis can overemphasize the role of language and thus become idealist, what I find valuable in this approach is its insistence that possession of socialist policies is of little use if these are not articulated in relation to the conceptions of actual (rather than potential) subjects. The Left can only gain support if it learns to articulate its concerns in terms of the cultural forms which people experience as their own common sense. Politics is as much about learning as it is about teaching.

There is a lot of work to do.

Notes

Introduction: Education and Textbooks

1 This theme will be fully developed in chapter 8, but here it should be noted that the process of socialization includes a conflict over the control of the young. In the course of such a conflict appeals to legitimating ideologies are made and agencies developed. The growth and extension of the practice *in loco parentis* is an example of this. Ideologie , then, are not just belief systems but practices. It has been suggested that many of the apparent parental rights (for example, to have one's children educated) were invented by the state when it began a new programme of social control through mass compulsory education. See JENNY SHAW, 'In loco parentis: A relationship between parent, state and child', in ROGER DALE et al. (Eds), *Education and the State, Volume 2: Politics, Patriarchy and Practice*, Lewes, Falmer Press, 1981, p. 267.

2 PAUL CORRIGAN, *Schooling the Smash Street Kids*, London, Macmillan, 1979, pp. 30–43.

3 See, for example, RICHARD JOHNSON, 'Really useful knowledge: Radical education and working-class culture 1790–1848', in JOHN CLARKE, CHAS CRITCHER and RICHARD JOHNSON (Eds), *Working-Class Culture: Studies in History and Theory*, London, Hutchison, 1979.

4 For a discussion of these issues see MICHAEL W. APPLE, *Ideology and Curriculum*, London, Routledge and Kegan Paul, 1979, p. 87. A common assumption is the primary importance of the separate individual. I will show how individualism is taken for granted on many teacher training courses in chapter 1.

5 See BRIAN FAY, *Social Theory and Political Practice*, London, George Allen and Unwin, 1974, p. 27.

6 Textbooks not only express the dominant groups' ideologies, they also help to form attitudes in support of their social position. But, of course, it is not as simple as this. We need to take account of the use to which a particular text is put, its function within a particular conjuncture, its relation to particular students. A textbook should not be considered in isolation from the historical conditions of its production and consumption, its insertion into a context of discourses in struggle. The meanings of a text will also be constructed differently depending on the discourses (knowledges, resistances) brought to bear on the text by the reader.

7 See JEAN ANYON, 'Ideology and United States history textbooks', in ROGER DALE et al. (Eds), *op. cit.*, p. 33.

Chapter 1   Ideology and Schooling

1 GEORG LUKÁCS, *History and Class Consciousness. Studies in Marxist Dialectics*, London, Merlin Press, 1971.

2 LOUIS ALTHUSSER and ETIENNE BALIBAR, *Reading Capital*, London, New Left Books, 1970, p. 94.

3 A useful way of beginning the study of new concepts is by looking them up in RAYMOND WILLIAMS, *Keywords. A Vocabulary of Culture and Society*, London, Fontana, 1976. This book explores the development and meaning of a hundred or so words which deal with strong feelings or important ideas. It shows how many crucial meanings have been shaped by a dominant class. One way in which a class tries to enforce its own uses of words as 'correct' is through dictionaries. The *Oxford English Dictionary*, for example, which was made from the 1880s to the 1920s, was very influential in the ideological process of 'fixing' the meaning of many keywords.

4 The fundamental questions about ideology are these: Does ideology have a negative or positive meaning? Is it mere illusion, false consciousness, a necessary deception which somehow distorts people's understandings of social reality? Or is it the expression of a world-view of a class? Secondly, is ideology subjective, a deformation of consciousness, which somehow is unable to grasp reality as it is? Or is it objective, in which case it is not the subject that distorts reality, but reality itself which deceives the subject. Thirdly, is ideology one part of the superstructure or is it co-extensive with the whole cultural sphere? Fourthly, is ideology the antithesis of science, that is to say, irrational and false? (Will ideology vanish when the scientific method is correctly applied?) Or, are both ideology *and* science the outcome of the originating class? According to this view, ideology cannot be overcome by science, and science itself may become ideological. See JORGE LARRAIN, *The Concept of Ideology*, London, Hutchinson, 1979, p. 14.

5 For studies on LUKÁCS, GRAMSCI, SARTRE, and ALTHUSSER see *Western Marxism. A Critical Reader*, edited by New Left Review, New Left Books, 1977. See also PERRY ANDERSON, *Considerations on Western Marxism*, London, New Left Books, 1976.

6 LOUIS ALTHUSSER, 'Ideology and ideological state apparatuses', in *Lenin and Philosophy and Other Essays*, London, New Left Books, 1971. The above paper is also in B.R. COSIN (Ed.), *Education: Structure and Society*, Harmondsworth, Penguin Books, 1972.

7 LOUIS ALTHUSSER, *Lenin and Philosophy*, op. cit., p. 129.

8 ALTHUSSER's main concern is with the structuring of thought and consciousness through ideological processes. In his theory ideology becomes co-extensive with 'culture'. Is this definition too wide to be really useful? JORGE LARRAIN has a much tighter definition; he argues that for ideology to be present two conditions should be satisfied: the objective concealment of contradictions and the interest of the dominant class. See LARRAIN, *op. cit.*, p. 210. But perhaps LARRAIN's definition of ideology is too narrow?

9 LOUIS ALTHUSSER, 'Marxism and humanism', in *For Marx*, Harmondsworth, Penguin Books, 1969, p. 232. Engels had suggested that ideology would end when men and women realized their real life conditions; because they would then be in contact with reality and their consciousness would become genuinely scientific. This notion of the end of ideology involves the idea that a true

consciousness of social relations is possible. But what, Althusser asks, if social totalities do not exist in a form which is accessible to experience?

10 Some of the questions that can be asked about 'a theory of ideology in general' are: Is it not ahistorical? How can one study ideology as an immutable object of study across the various modes of production? Can one really begin with the abstraction of ideology in general and deduce the conditions of the concrete particular ideologies?

11 ALTHUSSER, 1971, *op. cit.*, p. 135.

12 ALTHUSSER has been considerably influenced by GRAMSCI's thoughts on hegemony. For GRAMSCI hegemony is the ability of a class to assume a moral and intellectual leadership over the other classes without resorting to coercion. For the structuralist appropriation by ALTHUSSER of GRAMSCI see STUART HALL, BOB LUMLEY, GREGOR MCLENNAN, 'Politics and ideology: Gramsci', in Centre for Contemporary Cultural Studies, *On Ideology*, London, Hutchinson, 1978.

13 ALTHUSSER, 1971, *op. cit.*, p. 127. It is interesting to note the many similarities between Althusser's remarks about the functions of schools and the views of Bowles and Gintis. These American political economists argue that schools foster inequality through the ostensible meritocratic manner by which they reward and promote students and allocate them to positions in the production process. SAMUEL BOWLES and HERBERT GINTIS, *Schooling in Capitalist America*, London, Routledge and Kegan Paul, 1976.

14 ALTHUSSER, *op. cit.*, 1971, p. 147.

15 *Ibid.*, p. 138. In some secondary schools the methods of social control include the repeated use of threats and accusation, verbal abuse, insult, intimidation, incitement to racial hatred, the continual monitoring of pupils, various forms of regimentation, detention, suspension, exclusion and expulsion.

16 A sociological study has yet to be done of schoolteachers and schools as represented in drama, the novel and film. This would entail a reading, amongst others, of BRONTË, *Villette, Jane Eyre*; DICKENS, *Hard Times, Nicholas Nickleby, David Copperfield*; D.H. LAWRENCE, *The Rainbow*; JAMES JOYCE, *A Portrait of the Artist as a Young Man*; TERENCE RATTIGAN, *The Browning Version*; JAMES HILTON, *Goodbye Mr. Chips*; EDWARD BRAITHWAITE, *To Sir with Love*.

17 See GREGOR MCLENNAN, VICTOR MOLINA, ROY PETERS, 'Althusser's theory of ideology', in CCCS, *On Ideology, op. cit.*, p. 77.

18 Writing about Althusser, Richard Johnson comments: 'Dominant ideology, organized especially through apparatuses like schools, works with all the certainty usually ascribed to natural or biological processes. We are returned to a very familiar model of one-dimensional control in which all sense of struggle or contradiction is lost.' RICHARD JOHNSON, 'Three problematics', in JOHN CLARKE, CHAS CRITCHER and RICHARD JOHNSON (Eds), *Working-Class Culture: Studies in History and Theory*, London, Hutchinson, 1979, p. 230. For other criticisms see NORMAN GERAS, 'Althusser's Marxism: An assessment', in *Western Marxism, op. cit.*, pp. 264–72; ALEX COLLINICOS, *Althusser's Marxism*, London, Pluto, 1976, pp. 96–101.

19 PAUL Q. HIRST, *On Law and Ideology*, London, Macmillan, 1979, p. 42.

20 E.P. THOMPSON, *The Poverty of Theory*, London, Merlin Press, 1979.

Chapter 2   History, Experience and Structure

1 Richard Johnson calls Edward Thompson and Raymond Williams 'culturalists'. See RICHARD JOHNSON, 'Culture and the historians', in JOHN CLARKE, CHAS CRITCHER and RICHARD JOHNSON (Eds), *Working-Class Culture: Studies in History and Theory*, London, Hutchinson, 1979, p. 68. I prefer to use the term humanist to draw attention to their similarities with the Lukácsian tradition.

2 E.P. THOMPSON, *The Making of the English Working Class*, Harmondsworth, Penguin Books, 1968, p. 213.

3 PERRY ANDERSON, *Arguments within English Marxism*, London, New Left Books, 1980, p. 18. This book is really about the arguments between Anderson and Thompson about their conflicting theoretical positions. It is a cogent defence of Althusserian theory from Thompson's attack on it in *The Poverty of Theory*. In Anderson's book arguments within English marxism are omitted; there is no mention of sex or race politics; the polemics in economics between the neo-Ricardian, the neo-Sraffian and the Capital-logic school are ignored. After defending Althusser from the charge of being a Stalinist, Anderson discusses socialist politics and appeals for non-sectarianism. I have given a rendering of Anderson's main arguments against Thompsonian humanism in the chapter — but what are Anderson's recommendations? He resorts to Trotsky and his concept of dual power and suggests that socialists should reassess populism and nationalism. In brief, he argues against reformism and supports the creation of a left-populist revolutionary politics.

4 ANDERSON, *op. cit.*, p. 26.

5 *Ibid.*, p. 29.

6 E.P. THOMPSON, *op. cit.*, pp. 9–10. The second quotation is from p. 939.

7 E.P. THOMPSON, *The Poverty of Theory and Other Essays*, London, Merlin Press, 1978, pp. 298–9. In this book, an onslaught on Althusserian marxism, Thompson asserts the primacy of historical practice and contends that history is the central area of marxism; historical materialism, in other words, forms a part of history. He believes that the concept 'mode of production' should be rejected, but how, then, could economists help historians? Moreover, Thompson has a notion of an abstract human subject advancing towards freedom, but this is a view challenged, as we shall see, by many French theorists who have made the concept of 'the human subject' problematic.

8 G.A. COHEN, *Karl Marx's Theory of History — A Defence*, London, Oxford University Press, 1979, pp. 73–5.

9 See, for example, TED BENTON, *Philosophical Foundations of the Three Sociologies*, London Routledge and Kegan Paul, 1977, esp. chapters 8 and 9.

10 KARL MARX, 'Preface to a Critique of Political Economy', in DAVID McLELLAN (Ed.), *Karl Marx: Selected Writings*, London, Oxford University Press, 1977, p. 388. This Preface of 1859 is lucidly analyzed by G.A. COHEN, *op. cit.*, pp. 134–42. He argues that the concept of structure must be retained because it is sometimes appropriate to explain phenomena by reference to the economic structure itself in abstraction from the processes enveloping it.

11 ANDERSON, *op. cit.*, p. 55.

12 THOMPSON, 1978, *op. cit.*, p. 254. Thompson is right that traditional marxism has little to say about sexuality, family forms, and so on. I also think that marxist theories of class have neglected to take into account social cleavages arising from

the basis of racial, linguistic, religious, and sexual differences. It is essential for
rigorous work to be done in these areas.

13 ANDERSON, *op. cit.*, p. 68.
14 *Ibid.*, p. 72. See the section 'Base and superstructure' in RAYMOND WILLIAMS,
   Marxism and Literature, London, Oxford University Press, 1977, pp. 75–82.
15 A work like STUART HALL *et al.*, *Policing the Crisis*, London, Macmillan, 1978, is
   an excellent exemplification of this. It shows that though ideology slides into
   every level of the social structure, acting as a kind of cement of social cohesion, it
   is always related to the economic determinants.
16 RICHARD JOHNSON, 'Three problematics', in JOHN CLARKE, CHAS CRITCHER and
   RICHARD JOHNSON (Eds), *Working-Class Culture: Studies in History and
   Theory*, London, Hutchinson, 1979.

Chapter 3   Literature, Ideology and Schooling

1 TERRY EAGLETON, *Criticism and Ideology*, London, New Left Books, 1976, p.
   21. Works of Williams' first phase include *Reading and Criticism* and *Drama
   from Ibsen to Eliot*.
2 F.R. LEAVIS was the editor of *Scrutiny* (1932–53) which refashioned and yet at
   the same time reproduced the dominant ideology: liberal humanism. The journal
   was anti-democratic. Though it stressed the supremely civilizing discipline of
   literature, it ignored the majority of people who had no access to it. See FRANCIS
   MULHERN, *The Moment of Scrutiny*, London, New Left Books, 1981.
3 Quoted in EAGLETON, *op. cit.*, p. 22.
4 EAGLETON, *op. cit.*, p. 26. Works of Williams' second phase include *Culture and
   Society 1780–1950*, Harmondsworth, Penguin, 1961 and *The Long Revolution*,
   Harmondsworth, Penguin, 1965.
5 RAYMOND WILLIAMS, *Marxism and Literature*, London, Oxford University
   Press, 1977, p. 81.
6 Quoted in EAGLETON, *op. cit.*, p. 28.
7 RAYMOND WILLIAMS, *Culture and Society*, *op. cit.*, p. 289.
8 EAGLETON, *op. cit.*, p. 28.
9 Williams has been gently rebuked by some New Left Reviewers for his tendency
   to deny or discount the causal priority of the economic system, the gaping
   absence of Marx in *Culture and Society*, his curious lack of concern with
   nationalism and imperialism. They distrust his notion of community and are
   sceptical of 'the long revolution' (which probably means 'slow evolution'). See
   RAYMOND WILLIAMS, *Politics and Letters: Interviews with New Left Review*,
   London, New Left Books, 1979.
10 Some marxists believe that valuable literature is that which reflects social reality.
   Georg Lukács was antagonistic towards this sort of reflectionist position. He said
   that if we take this simple view of the relation between a work of art and reality,
   the reflection of reality in its immediately apprehensible form may be either
   insufficient or indeed illusory. Lukács argued that the task of the writer is to look
   beneath the surface appearance and discern the underlying movements. Hence his
   attack on naturalism which, it was said, simply reflects the appearance of things as
   they are, the immediately accessible reality. It should be added that Lukács and
   others of his school see literary texts as wholes which act as tokens, standing for

wider social situations and forces. This humanist view stresses the *unity* of a work of art, the world vision to which it corresponds, and the relations between this world vision and the social classes of which it is an expression. Critics such as Lukács favour classic (bourgeois) realism as the form for socialist novels. And so their main limitation is this: they are interested in *what* a text says, but not *how* it comes to have meaning. See GEORG LUKÁCS, *Realism in Our Time*, London, Harper and Row, 1964.

11 See, for example, RAYMOND WILLIAMS, 'Marxism, structuralism and literary analysis', in *New Left Review*, no. 129, September–October 1981.

12 The peculiarities of the English include a marked resistance to theoretical discourse; a ready recourse to empiricism; a preference for literary rather than sociological report; and a reluctance to subsume individual experience within more general categories. See E.P. THOMPSON, 'The peculiarities of the English', in *The Poverty of Theory and Other Essays*, London, Merlin Press, 1978.

13 For a lucid introduction to these writers I can recommend TERRY EAGLETON, *Marxism and Literary Criticism*, London, Methuen, 1976; more advanced students should read FREDRIC JAMESON, *Marxism and Form*, Princeton, N.J., Princeton University Press, 1971.

14 PIERRE MACHEREY, *A Theory of Literary Production*, London, Routledge and Kegan Paul, 1978, p. 68.

15 TERRY EAGLETON, 1976, *op. cit.*, p. 44. A limitation of Eagleton's schema, which he now concedes, is that it does not sufficiently consider the nature of the act which writing presupposes, and which 'completes' it: the act of reading.

16 *Ibid.*, p. 54. For a superb description of cultural domination and the struggle in language see BRIAN FRIEL, *Translations*, London, Faber and Faber, 1980. The play is about English troops making the first Ordinance Survey map in nineteenth-century Ireland. They are anglicizing all the place names and they meet with the collaboration and resistance of the oppressed. It depicts the lives of the peasants (of all ages) who, after a hard day's work, go to study in the 'hedge schools'. The teaching was in vernacular Gaelic, and the peasants attained a high degree of proficiency of the Latin and Greek classics. These schools were 'absorbed' in 1831 when the imperialist power introduced a state system of education in which all instruction was in English.

17 PIERRE MACHEREY, *op. cit.*, p. 85.

18 The increasing centralization and power of the school is discussed in MICHEL FOUCAULT, *Discipline and Punish*, London, Allen Lane, 1977, pp. 135–228.

19 There are about 2400 registered independent schools in Britain; the largest and most important of them are the public schools. In England and Wales there are about 460 public schools, and most of them are single-sex schools. At the time of writing this note (1982), the combined tuition and boarding fees are on average £2600 a year.

20 Terry Eagleton comments: 'I wonder whether your absolutely correct stress on the complexity of the "product" doesn't argue for the need for another category "Pupil Ideology" alongside "Teacher Ideology"? After all one could claim that the existent ideology of the pupil is a crucial constituent of the process of production. Have you considered this?' For the relationship between class and language see BASIL BERNSTEIN, *Class, Codes and Control*, London, Routledge and Kegan Paul, 1973; for the notion of 'cultural capital' see PIERRE BOURDIEU and J.C. PASSERON, *Reproduction*, London, Sage, 1977; SAMUEL BOWLES and

HERBERT GINTIS, *Schooling in Capitalist America*, London, Routledge and Kegan Paul, 1977. For the development of their ideas on education since the above book see ROGER DALE *et al.* (Eds), *Education and the State, Volume 1: Schooling and the National Interest*, Lewes, Falmer Press, 1981, p. 45.

21 RENÉE BALIBAR and D. LAPORTE, *Les Français fictifs*, Paris, Hachette, 1974, and *Le Français national*, Paris, Hachette, 1974.

22 But, of course, there are challenges. New approaches in marxism/structuralism question the division of labour of the classical disciplines. For example, the row at Cambridge University (the McCabe affair) was not a polemic between academics about method, but was a crisis of the object — the autonomy of 'English literature' itself.

23 RAYMOND WILLIAMS, 'Base and superstructure on Marxist cultural theory', in ROGER DALE *et al.* (Eds), *Schooling and Capitalism: A Sociological Reader*, London, Routledge and Kegan Paul, 1976, p. 205.

Chapter 4   Structuralism, Literature and Cultural Studies

1 TERENCE HAWKES, *Structuralism and Semiotics*, London, Methuen, 1977, is an extremely useful account, and I have drawn upon it in what follows.

2 JONATHAN CULLER, *Saussure*, London, Fontana/Collins, 1976, p. 35.

3 EDWARD SAPIR, *Selected Writings in Language Culture and Personality*, Berkeley, University of California Press, 1949, p. 162.

4 A good introduction is EDMUND LEACH, *Lévi-Strauss*, London, Fontana/Collins, 1970. LÉVI-STRAUSS, *Structural Anthropology*, Harmondsworth, Penguin Books, 1972, is a collection of useful essays, especially chapters 2 and 4 on linguistics and anthropology and chapter 11 on myth.

5 For a treatment of myth as an orchestra score see LÉVI-STRAUSS, *Structural Anthropology*, *op. cit.*, p. 212. An insightful exposition of the method is given in C.R. BADCOCK, *Lévi-Strauss: Structuralism and Sociological Theory*, London, Hutchinson, 1975, pp. 56–60.

6 STUART HALL *et al.* (Eds), *Culture, Media, Language*, London, Hutchinson, 1980, p. 32.

7 See MIRIAM GLUCKSMANN, 'The structuralism of Lévi-Strauss and Althusser' in JOHN REX (Ed.), *Approaches to Sociology*, London, Routledge and Kegan Paul, 1974, p. 243.

8 TONY BENNETT, *Formalism and Marxism*, London, Methuen, 1979, p. 19.

9 Some research needs to be done on the similarities and differences between the following concepts: defamiliarization (Shklovsky), making strange (Schutz), making problematic (Garfinkel), theorizing/reformulating the self (Blum and McHugh), and de-reification.

10 CATHERINE BELSEY, *Critical Practice*, London, Methuen, 1980, p. 7.

11 See LOUIS ALTHUSSER, *For Marx*, Harmondsworth, Penguin Books, 1969, p. 166; PIERRE MACHEREY, *A Theory of Literary Production*, London, Routledge and Kegan Paul, 1978, p. 137.

12 BELSEY, *op. cit.*, p. 91.

13 ROLAND BARTHES, *Writing Degree Zero*, London, Cape, 1967.

14 It may be remembered that Saussure said that the sound image (the signifier) and the concept (the signified) constitute the linguistic sign. In a similar way Barthes has suggested that in myth the signifier should be called form, the signified should be called the concept, and that the third term should be called signification. See ROLAND BARTHES, *Mythologies*, London, Paladin/Granada Publishing, 1972. pp. 114–17.

15 In Barthes' view realism is produced by a certain use of language. Realism stresses the product and not the production — all that matters is the illusion, the content, the story. Imitation is the basis of realist literature. Barthes has demonstrated how language produces the realist text as natural in his book *S/Z*, London, Cape, 1974. He identifies five essential codes for reading a text and suggests that there are three major forms of exchange by which society reproduces itself: language, sexuality and economics. Each of these requires a fixed positionality: addressor-addressee, masculine-feminine, buyer-seller.

16 ROLAND BARTHES, *Critical Essays*, Evanston, Northwestern University Press, 1972.

17 Semiology and semiotics refer to the same discipline. Semiology was conceived by Saussure, but at the same time the American C.S. Peirce conceived what he called semiotics. And so Europeans often use the former term, Anglo-Saxons the latter. See PIERRE GUIRARD, *Semiology*, London, Routledge and Kegan Paul, 1975, p. 2.

18 DICK HEBDIGE, *Subculture: The Meaning of Style*, London, Methuen, 1979. In Hebdige's view working-class subcultures are a series of mediated responses to the presence in Britain of black people.

19 CLAUDE LÉVI-STRAUSS, *The Savage Mind*, London, Weidenfeld and Nicholson, 1966. For a discussion of the contradictions in Lévi-Strauss' thought concerning the nature-culture distinction and *bricolage* from a post-structuralist position see JACQUES DERRIDA, 'Structure, sign and play in the discourse of the human sciences', in *Writing and Difference*, London, Routledge and Kegan Paul, 1978, pp. 283–6.

20 PAUL WILLIS, *Profane Culture*, London, Routledge and Kegan Paul, 1978.

21 JOHN CLARKE and TONY JEFFERSON, 'Working-class youth cultures', in GEOFF. MUNGHAM and GEOFF. PEARSON (Eds), *Working-Class Youth Culture*, London, Routledge and Kegan Paul, 1976, p. 156; see also STUART HALL *et al.* (Eds), *Resistance through Rituals*, London, Hutchinson, 1976.

22 ANGELA McROBBIE, 'Working-class girls and the culture of femininity', in Women's Studies Group, *Women Take Issue*, London, Hutchinson, 1978.

23 CCCS, Education Group, *Unpopular Education*, London, Hutchinson, 1982, p. 160.

24 HEBDIGE, *op. cit.*, p. 94.

25 BARTHES, *Mythologies*, *op. cit.*, p. 151; see also BARTHES, *Image — Music — Text*, translated by STEPHEN HEATH, London, Fontana, 1977.

26 PAUL WILLIS, *Learning to Labour*, Farnborough, Saxon House, 1977. Willis has shown that cultures of resistance sometimes actually reinforce rather than erode existing structures.

Chapter 5 The Undermining of Structuralism

1 SEBASTIANO TIMPANARO, *On Materialism*, London, New Left Books, 1975, p. 137.
2 *Ibid.*, p. 157.
3 TONY BENNETT, *Formalism and Marxism*, London, Methuen, 1979, p. 72.
4 The Russian marxist Mikhail Bakhtin stressed the idea that language is an arena of class struggle; his views are outlined in chapter 11.
5 See D.C. WOOD, 'An introduction to Derrida', in *Radical Philosophy*, no. 21, Spring 1979; see also JOHN STURROCK (Ed.), *Structuralism and Since; From Lévi-Strauss to Derrida*, London, Oxford University Press, 1979.
6 There is no ultimate meaning; every signifier refers to another signifier endlessly. See JACQUES DERRIDA, *Speech and Phenomena*, Evanston, Northwestern University Press, 1973; *Writing and Difference*, London, Routledge and Kegan Paul, 1981.
7 For a most lucid discussion of issues raised in this section see CHRISTOPHER NORRIS, *Deconstruction: Theory and Practice*, London, Methuen, 1982.
8 JACQUES DERRIDA, 'The dangerous supplement', in *Of Grammatology*, Baltimore, Johns Hopkins University Press, 1977.
9 Derrida rejects the Althusserian idea of revolution as a complete discontinuity, a rupture, and suggests that in a revolution there are continuities as well. Many years ago in an article in the Parisian journal *Tel Quel* JACQUES DERRIDA wrote that his encounter with marxism was yet to come. This encounter has still not taken place. Since then he has said that his silence is not to be taken as neutrality, and he has refused to join the reactionary 'New Philosophers'.
10 'Much structuralist analysis is formalist in the sense of separating form and content and giving form priority.' RAYMOND WILLIAMS, *Keywords. A Vocabulary of Culture and Society*, London, Fontana, 1976, p. 258.
11 Eagleton has argued that Derrida is in the tradition of a long line of philosophers who are against philosophy: Heidegger, Nietzsche, Wittgenstein. The work of Wittgenstein is, in some ways, similar to that of Derrida, but is also a corrective to it. Wittgenstein noted that there was vagueness in our use of language, that there was a necessary ambiguity in social rules. And so he argued that a certain amount of indeterminacy is necessary in life for social interaction to take place. Now, the post-structuralists say there is no last definition; there is a permanent gap between any text and any unitary 'meaning'. In contrast, Wittgenstein is valuable in that he reminds us that 'doubting must have an end', and that the signified is embedded in cultural convention, 'forms of life'. It has to be conceded that this ahistorical concept needs to be sharpened, but it should be noted that when Wittgenstein said that philosophy leaves everything as it is, he did not mean that philosophy is pointless, but rather that if changes are desired, then those changes have to occur at the level of 'forms of life', not from philosophy itself. In the context of class struggle it is necessary to use such terms as 'certainty', 'determinacy', 'science', 'theory', 'reality', 'meaning' and 'truth'. TERRY EAGLETON discusses DERRIDA in 'Marxism and deconstruction', an essay in *Walter Benjamin or towards a Revolutionary Criticism*, London, Verso/New Left Books, 1981, pp. 131–42.
12 ROLAND BARTHES quoted in MICHAEL LANE (Ed.), *Structuralism: A Reader*, London, Cape, 1970, p. 37.

13 Derrida, Lacan, Foucault are the names of problems, not 'authors' of doctrines. Their work is interrelated, but in no way homogeneous. For a useful exposition of their work see the introduction and part one of ROBERT YOUNG (Ed.), *Untying the Text: A Post-Structuralist Reader*, London, Routledge and Kegan Paul, 1981.

Chapter 6   The Structuring of Subjectivity

1 SAMUEL BOWLES and HERBERT GINTIS, *Schooling in Capitalist America*, London, Routledge and Kegan Paul, 1976, p. 131.

2 MICHAEL W. APPLE, *Ideology and Curriculum*, London, Routledge and Kegan Paul, 1979, pp. 51–7.

3 See MADELEINE MACDONALD, 'Schooling and the reproduction of class and gender relations', in ROGER DALE *et al.* (Eds), *Education and the State, Volume 2: Politics, Patriarchy and Practice*, Lewes, Falmer Press, 1981, p. 165.

4 JACQUES LACAN, *Écrits*, London, Tavistock, 1977, p. 159. It should be noted that Lacan rejects the term 'individual', which has an implication of self-sufficiency, and uses the term 'subject' because of the connotation of being 'thrown under' in a pre-existing process.

5 SIGMUND FREUD, *The Interpretation of Dreams*; *The Psychopathology of Everyday Life*; *Jokes and Their Relation to the Unconscious*; These books are volumes 4, 5, and 6 in the Pelican Freud Library.

6 ROMAN JAKOBSON, 'Linguistics and poetics', in RICHARD AND FERNANDE DE GEORGE (Eds), *The Structuralists: From Marx to Lévi-Strauss*, New York, Anchor Books, 1972. See also JAKOBSON, 'On Russian fairy tales', in MICHAEL LANE (Ed.), *Structuralism: A Reader*, London, Cape, 1970. For Lacan's linking of metaphor with condensation, and metonymy with displacement see *Écrits*, *op. cit.*, p. 160.

7 'If I have said that the unconscious is the discourse of the Other, it is in order to indicate the beyond in which the recognition of desire is bound up with the desire for recognition.' JACQUES LACAN, *Écrits*, *op. cit.*, p. 72.

8 LACAN, *op. cit.*, p. 166.

9 ROSALIND COWARD and JOHN ELLIS, *Language and Materialism. Developments in Semiology and the Theory of the Subject*, London, Routledge and Kegan Paul, 1977.

10 *Ibid.*, p. 78. I think Jonathan Rée's review of *Language and Materialism* is too harsh. He sees the book as advocating a *mélange* of structuralism and psychoanalysis as the highest form of marxism. In his view the book is part of a fashionable ephemeral importation, a movement which testifies to the real need for an alternative to bourgeois organizations of knowledge. See JONATHAN RÉE, 'Marxist modes', in *Radical Philosophy*, no. 23, Winter 1979, p. 11.

11 *Language and Materialism*, *op. cit.*, p. 80.

12 *Ibid.*, p. 155.

13 *Ibid.*, p. 91.

14 KARL MARX, 'Theses on Feuerbach, III', in CHRIS, ARTHUR (Ed.), *The German Ideology*, London, Lawrence and Wishart, 1970, p. 121.

15 Note the shift of interest in cultural studies from popular mass art to that of the avant-garde, from realism to modernism. Thus a link with the popular and the

pleasurable has been lost. The language of avant-garde art is based on a cultural and eductional apparatus to which the working class has little access.

16 COWARD and ELLIS, *op. cit.*, p. 43.

17 See the journal *Screen* which is obtainable from the Society for Education in Film and Television, 29 Old Compton Street, London, W1V 5PL.

18 See the essay 'Ideology and ideological state apparatuses', in LOUIS ALTHUSSER, *Lenin and Philosophy*, London, New Left Books, 1971, p. 160.

19 Compare FERDINAND DE SAUSSURE, *Course in General Linguistics*, London, Fontana/Collins, 1974, pp. 66–7, and JACQUES LACAN, *Écrits, op. cit.*, p. 149.

20 LACAN, *op. cit.*, p. 86.

21 From *The Complete Introductory Lectures on Psychoanalysis*, p. 544, quoted by ANDREW COLLIER in 'Lacan, psychoanalysis and the left', in *International Socialism*, no. 7, Winter 1980.

22 Just as Lévi-Strauss has written of the exchange of women, Lacan interprets the phallus as the object of symbolic exchange within and between generations in the Western family. Juliet Mitchell and Coward and Ellis insist that the penis/phallus equation and the power structures which go with it are not necessarily universal but culturally and historically specific and therefore changeable, even within the terms of Lacan's theory. See JULIET MITCHELL, *Psychoanalysis and Feminism*, Harmondsworth, Penguin Books, 1974, pp. 402–3. For the influence of Lévi-Strauss on Lacan see ANTHONY WILDEN, *System and Structure: Essays in Communication and Exchange*, London, Tavistock, 1972, chapter 1. Having just completed the Lévi-Strauss Chapter, I have noticed the following binary oppositions in Lacan's work: absence, unpleasure / presence, gain in pleasure; discourse of the unconscious / discourse of the conscious; the true self / the self for others, the ego; infinity of desires, unrealizable because of social rules / finitude of demands, allowable by society; subversion of the ego / reinstatement of the id; I think (Descartes) / I wish (Freud); the static, unity of being / the contradictory, subject 'in process'.

23 TERRY LOVELL, *Pictures of Reality: Aesthetics, Politics and Pleasure*, London, British Film Institute, 1980, p. 46.

24 See STUART HALL's essay 'Recent developments in theories of language and ideology: A critical note', in STUART HALL *et al.* (Eds), *Culture, Media, Language*, London, Hutchinson, 1980, p. 160.

Chapter 7   The Post-Structuralism of Foucault

1 'Prison talk', *Radical Philosophy*, no. 16, Spring 1977.

2 MICHEL FOUCAULT, *The Archaeology of Knowledge*, London, Tavistock, 1972, p. 13.

3 MICHEL FOUCAULT, *The Order of Things*, London, Tavistock, 1970, pp. 261–2.

4 Quoted in ALAN SHERIDAN, *Michel Foucault: The Will to Truth*, London, Tavistock, 1980, p. 116. Sheridan's account of Foucault's work is extremely helpful, and I have drawn upon it.

5 MICHEL FOUCAULT, *Madness and Civilization*, London, Tavistock, 1967.

6 MICHEL FOUCAULT, *The Birth of the Clinic*, London, Tavistock, 1973, p. 195.

7 FOUCAULT, *The Order of Things, op. cit.*

8 *Ibid.*, pp. 127–8.

9 FOUCAULT, *The Archaeology of Knowledge, op. cit.*, p. 49.

10 MICHEL FOUCAULT, *L'Ordre du Discours*, Paris, Gallimard, 1971. 'The discourse on language' is included as an appendix to the American edition of *The Archaeology of Knowledge*, New York, Pantheon, 1972.

11 MICHEL FOUCAULT, 'Language, counter-memory, practice', in D.F. BOUCHARD (Ed.), *Selected Essays*, Oxford, Blackwell, 1977.

12 MICHEL FOUCAULT, *Discipline and Punish*, London, Allen Lane, 1977.

13 For a full discussion of *Discipline and Punish*, especially its relevance to schooling, see MADAN SARUP, *Education, State and Crisis*, London, Routledge and Kegan Paul, 1982, chapter 2.

14 MICHEL FOUCAULT, *The History of Sexuality, Volume One: An Introduction*, London, Allen Lane, 1979.

15 *Ibid.*, p. 59.

16 FOUCAULT, 1977, *op. cit.*, p. 27.

17 FOUCAULT, 1979, *op. cit.*, p. 93. For his views on power see pp. 92–6, and on how power and knowledge are joined together in discourse see pp. 100–2.

18 MICHEL FOUCAULT, 'The political function of the intellectual', in *Radical Philosophy*, no. 17, Summer 1977. This issue also contains a survey on Foucault's work by Colin Gordon, entitled 'Birth of the subject'.

19 VALERIE WALKERDINE, 'Piaget, cognitive development and the scientific pedagogy', in JULIAN HENRIQUES *et al.*, *Changing the Subject*, London, Tavistock, in press.

20 On Susan Isaacs see WILLEM VAN DER EYKEN (Ed.), *Education, the Child and Society: A Documentary History 1900–1973*, Harmondsworth, Penguin Books, 1973, pp. 290–5.

21 For Piaget's claims see MARGARET DONALDSON, *Children's Minds*, London, Croom Helm, 1978, pp. 129–45; MARGARET BODEN, *Piaget*, London, Fontana, 1979.

22 For example, the principles of Freudian analysis were used to deal with the problems of difficult adolescents by the American Homer Lane in the private, co-educational Dorset community 'The Little Commonwealth'. See VAN DER EYKEN, *op. cit.*, p. 175; for A.S. Neill on freedom see p. 321.

23 But one problem here is that teachers often feel threatened if their practices are analyzed critically without alternative practices being suggested.

24 NIKOLAS ROSE, 'The psychological complex: Mental measurement and social administration', in *Ideology and Consciousness*, no. 5, Spring 1979. Foucault's work is often discussed in *m/f*, obtainable from 22 Chepstow Crescent, London, W11; *I & C* is obtainable from Graham Burchell, Westminster College, North Hinksey, Oxford OX2 9AT.

25 Foucault's theory of power is discussed in BOB FINE, 'Struggles against discipline: The theory and politics of Michel Foucault', in *Capital and Class*, no. 9, Autumn 1979.

Chapter 8   The Family, State and Schooling

1 JACQUES DONZELOT, *The Policing of Families*, with a foreword by Gilles Deleuze, London, Hutchinson, 1980. For Donzelot the family is a concrete locus

where the discourses marxism, feminism and psychoanalysis meet. He is critical of all three discourses.

2 MICHEL FOUCAULT, *The History of Sexuality, Volume One: An Introduction*, Harmondsworth, Penguin Books, 1981, pp. 104–5.

3 See also the useful reader edited by CHRIS JENKS, *The Sociology of Childhood*, London, Batsford, 1982, which contains material by Ariés, Piaget, Barthes, Foucault and others.

4 DONZELOT, *op. cit.*, p. 79.

5 *Ibid.*, p. 89.

6 For an understanding of how the state uses the family in a variety of spheres to reproduce existing divisions and relations see MARY WILSON, *Women and the Welfare State*, London, Tavistock, 1977. She argues that social policy is simply one aspect of the capitalist state and social welfare policies amount to no less than the *state organization of domestic life*. A study that outlines the way the state, through educational policies, has regulated paternal and maternal relations with children in school and familial relations within schools is MIRIAM DAVID, *The State, the Family and Education*, London, Routledge and Kegan Paul, 1980.

7 DONZELOT, *op. cit.*, p. 133.

8 *Ibid.*, p. 149.

9 Donzelot emphasizes that this transformation of the family was effected by the active participation of women. For example, the woman was chosen by the medical and teaching professions to work in partnership with them in order to disseminate their principles, to win adherence to the new norms, within the home.

10 'After the Coservative government's return in 1970, there was an attempt to introduce methods of administration more familiar to business enterprises: programme analysis and review methods were favoured. In this system, objectives had to be defined, policy alternatives costed and measured for relative efficiency.' CCCS, Education Group, *Unpopular Education*, London, Hutchinson, 1981, p. 180.

11 As Pateman has remarked: 'when the ends of education cease to be consensual ... the claim to professional freedom logically collapses. For in such a situation there is no longer a neutral professional dealing in expertly assessable means.' See TREVOR PATEMAN, 'Accountability, values and schooling', in ROGER DALE *et al.* (Eds), *Education and the State, Volume 2: Politics, Patriarchy and Practice*, Lewes, Falmer Press, 1981, p. 382.

12 For a discussion of issues raised in this paragraph see MADAN SARUP, *Education, State and Crisis*, London, Routledge and Kegan Paul, 1982.

13 It has been argued that cuts in social welfare expenditures can amount to a disguised wage-cut. Cuts in education are not as direct or obvious as a reduction in one's take-home pay. See PAUL ADAMS, 'Social control or social wage: On the political economy of the "Welfare State"', in ROGER DALE *et al.* (Eds), *Politics, Patriarchy and Practice, op. cit.*, p. 231.

Chapter 9   Teachers: Class Position and Socialist Pedagogy

1 CCCS, Education Group, *Unpopular Education*, London, Hutchinson, 1981.

2 For a critique of the 'old' sociology of education see *Unpopular Education, op. cit.*, pp. 79–89.

3 Within this problematic can be placed the work of Hargreaves and Lacey, both of whom remain within the parameters of a social democratic politics of access. DAVID HARGREAVES, *Social Relations in the Secondary School*, London, Routledge and Kegan Paul, 1967; COLIN LACEY, *Hightown Grammar*, Manchester, Manchester University Press, 1970.

4 *Unpopular Education, op. cit.*, p. 215.

5 See ERIC HOBSBAWM *et al.*, *The Forward March of Labour Halted?*, London, New Left Books, 1981. Hobsbawm declares that after a century of constant progress the British Labour movement is now in crisis. Class and occupational structure have changed; one third of all workers consistently votes Tory. Should the Labour Party become not a class party but a people's party?

6 *Unpopular Education, op. cit.*, p. 249. The work of Ernesto Laclau is important here in that it deals with ideological meaning. It will be discussed in chapter 11.

7 My students have pointed out to me that the original fifty-page article (by DAN FINN, NEIL GRANT and RICHARD JOHNSON, 'Social Democracy, education and the crisis', in CCCS, *On Ideology*, London, Hutchinson, 1977) is in many ways much better than the full-length book.

8 *Unpopular Education, op. cit.*, p. 75.

9 *Ibid.*, p. 244.

10 MAURICE KOGAN, *The Politics of Education*, Harmondsworth, Penguin Books, 1971, quoted in *Unpopular Education, op. cit.*, p. 88.

11 HARRY BRAVERMAN, *Labour and Monopoly Capitalism*, New York, Monthly Review Press, 1974.

12 ANTONIO GRAMSCI, 'The intellectuals', in *Selections from the Prison Notebooks*, edited by QUINTIN HOARE and GEOFFREY NOWELL SMITH, London, Lawrence and Wishart, 1971, p. 3.

13 ERNEST MANDEL, *Late Capitalism*, London, New Left Books, 1975, p. 270.

14 NICOS POULANTZAS, *Classes in Contemporary Capitalism*, London, New Left Books, 1975.

15 Barbara and John Ehrenreich have argued that Marx's two-class model (the bourgeoisie and proletariat) does not apply in monopoly-capitalist society because of the rapid growth of a new educated middle class: the Professional-Managerial Class. (These writers estimate that in the United States between 20 and 25 per cent of the population belong to this class: fifty million people.) There is antagonism between the PMC and the working class. But the contradiction in the USA is this: the Left is now predominantly drawn from the middle class. Both classes confront the capitalist class over the issue of ownership and control of the means of production. They confront each other over the issues of knowledge, skills, culture. BARBARA and JOHN EHRENREICH, 'The Professional-Managerial Class', in PAT WALKER (Ed.), *Between Labour and Capital*, Hassocks, Harvester Press, 1979, p. 12.

16 ERIK OLIN WRIGHT, 'Intellectuals and the class structure of capitalist society', in PAT WALKER (Ed.), *Between Labour and Capital, op. cit.*, p. 203. Much of what follows is indebted to Wright's analysis.

17 'The major control on the structuring of knowledge at the secondary level is the structuring of knowledge at the tertiary level, specifically the university. Only if there is a major change in the structuring of knowledge at this level can there be

effective code change at lower levels.' Basil Bernstein, *Class, Codes and Control, Vol. 3*, London, Routledge and Kegan Paul, 1975, p. 115.

18 Nevertheless, those who control the universities are usually very selective about whom they recruit, and by not providing permanent tenure they severely limit the autonomy of teachers. On the other hand, university teachers have many privileges. Sabbaticals, choice of working hours and freedom of expression on the job, virtually unknown outside the academic world, are rights which should be extended to everyone.

19 See Guglielmo Carchedi, 'The proletarianization of the employees', in Theo Nichols (Ed.), *Capital and Labour*, London, Fontana, 1980. See also the useful essays on 'Education and work', pp. 190–209.

20 Wright in Pat Walker (Ed.), *Between Labour and Capital, op. cit.*, p. 208.

21 Paulo Freire, *Pedagogy of the Oppressed*, Harmondsworth, Penguin Books, 1972, p. 46.

22 *Ibid.*, p. 59.

23 For a brief and clear introduction to the dialectic see the Foreword by Martin Nicolaus of Karl Marx, *Grundrisse*, Harmondsworth, Penguin Books, 1973, pp. 27–33. This discussion about 'traditional' and 'progressive' methods of teaching and the role of socialist pedagogy will be further developed in the next chapter.

24 Theodore Mills Norton and Bertell Ollman (Eds), *Studies in Socialist Pedagogy*, New York, Monthly Review Press, 1978, p. 15.

25 *Ibid.*, p. 217.

26 V.I. Lenin, 'The tasks of the Youth League' in *On Culture and Cultural Revolution*, Moscow, Progress Publishers, 1970.

27 This is the view, for example, of Carmen Claudin-Urondo, *Lenin and the Cultural Revolution*, Hassocks, Harvester Press, 1977.

Chapter 10 Education and Social Change: The work of Gramsci

1 James Joll, *Gramsci*, London, Fontana, 1977, p. 72. Besides Croce, the main influences on Gramsci's thinking were Hegel (state and civil society), Machiavelli (*The Prince*), Marx (base and superstructure), Labriola (philosophy of praxis), Luxemburg (the spontaneous uprising), and Lenin (Jacobinism).

2 Quintin Hoare and Geoffrey Nowell Smith (Eds), *Selections from the Prison Notebooks of Antonio Gramsci*, London, Lawrence and Wishart, 1971, p. 350.

3 *Ibid.*, p. 325.

4 *Ibid.*, p. 36.

5 *Ibid.*, p. 37.

6 *Ibid.*, p. 327.

7 *Ibid.*, p. 330.

8 *Ibid.*, p. 340.

9 See George Mardle, 'Power, tradition, and change: Educational implications of the thought of Antonio Gramsci', in Denis Gleeson (Ed.), *Identity and Structure: Issues in the Sociology of Eduction*, Driffield, Nafferton Books, 1977, p. 136.

10 See Herbert Gintis and Samuel Bowles, 'Contradiction and reproduction in

educational theory', in ROGER DALE *et al.*, *Education and the State, Volume 1: Schooling and the National Interest*, Lewes, Falmer Press, 1981.

11 HAROLD ENTWISTLE, *Antonio Gramsci: Conservative Schooling for Radical Politics*, London, Routledge and Kegan Paul, 1979, p. 85.

12 See MADAN SARUP, *Education, State and Crisis*, London, Routledge and Kegan Paul, 1982, pp. 1–13.

13 Compare, for example, MICHAEL F.D. YOUNG (Ed.), *Knowledge and Control*, London, Collier Macmillan, 1971, with MICHAEL F.D. YOUNG and GEOFFREY WHITTY (Eds), *Society, State and Schooling*, Lewes, Falmer Press, 1977.

14 ANTONIO GRAMSCI, 'Socialism and culture', in *Selections from Political Writings (1910–1920)*, edited by QUINTIN HOARE, London, Lawrence and Wishart, 1977, p. 10.

15 ENTWISTLE, *Antonio Gramsci, op. cit.*, p. 2.

16 GRAMSCI, *Prison Notebooks, op. cit.*, p. 144.

17 ENTWISTLE, *Antonio Gramsci, op. cit.*, p. 46.

18 *Ibid.*, p. 50.

19 *Ibid.*, p. 54.

20 *Ibid.*, p. 59.

21 *Ibid.*, p. 65.

22 PHILIP SIMPSON, 'The whalebone in the corset: Gramsci on education, culture and change' in *Screen Education*, no. 28, Autumn 1978.

23 For a discussion of work see ALFRED SCHMIDT, *The Concept of Nature in Marx*, London, New Left Books, 1971.

24 ENTWISTLE, *Antonio Gramsci, op. cit.*, p. 54.

25 *Ibid.*, p. 148.

26 *Ibid.*, p. 167.

27 For some differing recent interpretations see CHANTAL MOUFFE (Ed.), *Gramsci and Marxist Theory*, London, Routledge and Kegan Paul, 1979.

28 For discussion of issues raised in this paragraph see JOHN MERRINGTON, 'Theory and practice in Gramsci's Marxism', in *Western Marxism: A Critical Reader*, London, New Left Books, 1977; RAYMOND WILLIAMS, *Marxism and Literature*, London, Oxford University Press, 1977, p. 108.

29 See CARL BOGGS, *Gramsci's Marxism*, London, Pluto Press, 1976, p. 39.

30 ANTONIO GRAMSCI, *Quaderni del Carcere*, p. 1638, quoted in JOLL, *op. cit.*, p. 99 [my emphasis]. The best illustration of this point is STUART HALL *et al.*, *Policing the Crisis*, London, Macmillan, 1978.

31 GRAMSCI, *Prison Notebooks, op. cit.*, p. 350.

32 *Ibid.*, p. 334.

33 *Ibid.*, p. 340.

34 For an examination of the relationship between the party and the working class in the work of Marx, Lenin, Luxemburg, Trotsky and Gramsci see JOHN MOLYNEUX, *Marxism and the Party*, London, Pluto Press, 1978.

35 PERRY ANDERSON, *Considerations on Western Marxism*, London, New Left Books, 1976, pp. 54–5.

36 GRAMSCI, *Prison Notebooks, op. cit.*, p. 238. In a highly critical text Perry Anderson has pointed out the ambiguities and the shifting positions concerning the relationship between state and civil society in Gramsci's thought: In the West, is the state only an outer surface of civil society? Is the state in a balanced relationship with civil society? Is the state a massive structure that cancels the

autonomy of civil society? Let me rephrase these questions: Does the state, for Gramsci, contrast with civil society? Does the state encompass civil society? Or is the state identical with civil society? See PERRY ANDERSON, 'The antinomies of Antonio Gramsci', in *New Left Review*, no. 100, Novermber 1976 — January 1977.

37 JOLL, *op. cit.*, p. 112.

38 But for a stimulating essay on the structuralist appropriation of Gramsci (by Althusser and Poulantzas) see STUART HALL, BOB LUMLEY, GREGOR McLENNAN, 'Politics and ideology: Gramsci', in *On Ideology*, London, Hutchison, 1978.

Chapter 11 Review

1 Traditional notions of authorship are being challenged by a stress on the structural conditions of artistic production. See JANET WOLFF, *The Social Production of Art*, London, Macmillan, 1981, chapter 6.

2 SEBASTIANO TIMPANARO, *On Materialism*, London, New Left Books, 1975, p. 189. Similar criticisms of structuralism were also made by Macherey as early as 1965. He noted that structuralism presupposes the traditional notion of harmony and unity and that works, in that perspective, are never related to the material conditions of their production. Besides questioning the unproblematized transference of knowledge from one discipline (linguistics) to another, he attacked structuralism for its ahistoricism. See PIERRE MACHEREY, *A Theory of Literary Production*, London, Routledge and Kegan Paul, 1978, pp. 136–56.

3 TIMPANARO, *On Materialism*, op. cit., p. 192.

4 I am thinking of a reader like RICHARD DE GEORGE and FERNANDE DE GEORGE (Eds), *The Structuralists: From Marx to Lévi-Strauss*, New York, Doubleday Anchor, 1972.

5 Though structuralism may always seek the system behind the event, it cannot for all that dispense with the individual subject. Culler remarks, 'He may no longer be the origin of meaning, but meaning must move through him.... And though the individual may not originate or even control this process, it takes place through him.' See JONATHAN CULLER, *Structuralist Poetics: Structuralism, Linguistics and the Study of Literature*, London, Routledge and Kegan Paul, 1975, p. 30.

6 C.R. BADCOCK, *Lévi-Strauss: Structuralism and Sociological Theory*, London, Hutchinson, 1975, p. 109.

7 TIMPANARO, *op. cit.*, p. 182.

8 *Ibid.*, p. 187.

9 V. VOLOŠINOV, *Marxism and the Philosophy of Language*, New York, Seminar Press, 1973; VOLOŠINOV, *Freudianism: A Marxist Critique*, New York, Academic Press, 1976; BAKHTIN, *The Formal Method in Literary Scholarship*, Baltimore, 1978; BAKHTIN, *The Dialogical Imagination*, Texas, 1981.

10 It is significant that the work that was first translated and became influential in Britain was the work of the early formalists, and that the later, more social and historical work of people like Bakhtin and Mukarovsky is still less familiar. See RAYMOND WILLIAMS, 'Marxism, structuralism and literary analysis', in *New Left*

Review, no. 129, September-October 1981, p. 61.

11 CHRISTINE GLEDHILL, 'Recent developments in film criticism', in *Quarterly Review of Film Studies*, vol. 3, no. 4, Fall 1978; quoted in CCCS, *Culture, Media, Language*, London, Hutchinson, 1980, p. 170.

12 For a discussion of this point see TERRY LOVELL, *Pictures of Reality: Aesthetics, Politics and Pleasure*, London, British Film Institute Publishing, 1980, p. 82.

13 See ELLEN MEIKSINS WOOD, 'The separation of the economic and political in capitalism', in *New Left Review*, no. 127, May-June, 1981, p. 95.

14 G.A. COHEN, *Karl Marx's Theory of History: A Defence*, London, Oxford University Press, 1978, p. 73. Cohen points out that it was Marx's perception of structure and its importance which led him to claim that he had discovered the *anatomy* of society.

15 See PETER DEWS, 'The New Philosophers and the end of leftism', in *Radical Philosophy*, no. 24, Spring 1980.

16 B.-H. LÉVY, *La Barbarie à Visage humain*, Paris, Grasset, 1977.

17 As Peter Dews has pointed out, the modish Left in Britain has now started stressing the plurality and specificity of social practices against class analysis (termed 'class essentialism') and to suspect marxism of being a dangerously totalizing discourse. For a discussion of the important influence of Foucault on the 'New Philosophers' see PETER DEWS, 'Nouvelle philosophie and Foucault', in *Economy and Society*, vol. 8, no. 2, May 1979.

18 See CHANTAL MOUFFE (Ed.), *Gramsci and Marxist Theory*, op. cit., pp. 54–5. But I take issue with her when she asserts that 'it is quite remarkable to see the extraordinary way in which some contemporary research — such as that of Foucault or Derrida which brings out a completely new conception of politics — converges with Gramsci's thought' (p. 201). Foucault and other post-structuralists have certainly brought about new concepts in social theory, but I think their work has little in common with Gramsci's view of revolutionary struggle.

19 See particularly the essays on 'Fascism and ideology' and 'Towards a theory of populism', in ERNESTO LACLAU, *Politics and Ideology in Marxist Theory*, London, New Left Books, 1977. For a useful discussion of Gramsci's work and its development by Laclau and Mouffe see BOB JESSOP, *The Capitalist State*, Oxford, Martin Robertson, 1980, pp. 191–210.

20 ANTONY CUTLER, BARRY HINDESS, PAUL HIRST, and ATHAR HUSSAIN, *Marx's 'Captial' and Capitalism Today*, London, Routledge and Kegan Paul, 1977. Hindess and Hirst are said to have 'deconstructed' marxism, but one could ask, so what? It could be argued that deconstruction is not about texts but about deconstructing the institutions that produce the texts. In the final analysis the question of method cannot be answered methodologically. The goals with which we are concerned are political.

21 For a discussion of these Gramscian concepts see PERRY ANDERSON, 'The antinomies of Antonio Gramsci', in *New Left Review*, no. 100, November 1976–January 1977.

22 Chantal Mouffe works closely with Laclau; see 'Hegemony and ideology in Gramsci', in CHANTAL MOUFFE (Ed.), *Gramsci and Marxist Theory*, op. cit., p. 195.

23 It is the multi-accentuality of the sign which makes it possible for discourse to become an arena of struggle. The signified is always being constituted and

reformed. But it should be noted that Laclau never refers to the psychoanalytic level; he makes no reference to the Lacanian hypothesis. Though Laclau is valuable in that he stresses ideological (processes and) struggle, there is an aspect of his work that troubles me. I appreciate the fact that he is against any essentialist notion of society and insists on a non-reductionist view. In his theory, however, there seem to be only discursive practices and politics. Politics implies contesting forces; it takes place in the field of the discursive. The discursive is defined as 'the ensemble of the phenomena in and through which social production of meaning takes place.' Every discourse has specific conditions of production. Every social practice is production of meaning. But the discursive is not a 'level'; Laclau contends that it is co-extensive with the social. What worries me is his affirmation of the priority of the discursive. There is, he writes, *an identity between society and discourse*. Even economic practice is seen as discourse. See ERNESTO LACLAU, 'Populist rupture and discourse', in *Screen Education*, no. 34, 1980, p. 87.

24 Laclau has suggested that the discourse of rupture can be found in Chartism, Mazzinism and the Jacobin tradition, and the discourse of integration in Disraeli, Bismarck and others. In the latter the discourse of difference is substituted for the discourse of antagonism. That is to say, capitalists and workers are considered as different but equally legitimate categories.

25 ERNESTO LACLAU and CHANTAL MOUFFE, 'Socialist strategy — Where next?' in *Marxism Today*, January 1981; ERNEST LACLAU and CHANTAL MOUFFE, *Hegemony and Socialist Strategy*, London, New Left Books, forthcoming.

Subject Index

Name Index

De George, R. and De George, F., 176 n
   6, 183 n 4
Deleuze, G., 109
Derrida, J., 65–70, 87, 112, 153, 174 n
   19, 175 n 6, n 8, n 9 and n 11, 176 n 13
Descartes, 78, 81, 88, 89
Dews, P., 184 n 15 and n 17
Dilthey, W., 8
Donaldson, M., 178 n 21
Donzelot, J., 103–12, 178–9 n 1, 179 n
   5, n 6, n 7–n 9
Douglas, J.W.B., 3, 114
Durkheim, E., 51, 73

Eagleton, T., 29, 30, 32, 33–7, 38, 43,
   147, 171 n 1, n 3, n 4, n 6 and n 8, 172
   n 13, n 15 and n 20, 175 n 11
Ehrenreich, B. and Ehrenreich, J.,
   119–20, 180 n 15
Ellis, J.
   see Coward and Ellis
Engels, F., 8, 10, 168 n 9
Entwistle, H., 134–8, 182 n 11, n 15, n
   17–n 21, n 24–n 26
Erikson, E., 74

Fay, B., 167 n 5
Fine, B., 178 n 25
Finn, D., *et al.*, 180 n 4
Floud, J.E., 114
Foucault, M., 45, 69–70, 81, 87–102,
   103, 109, 110, 111, 112, 157–8, 159,
   172 n 18, 176 n 13, 177–8, 179 n 2, 184
   n 18
Freire, P., 123, 160, 181 n 21 and n 22
Friel, B., 172 n 16
Freud, S., 12, 37, 45, 73–85, 152, 155,
   159, 176 n 5, 178 n 22

Gentile, G., 133
Geras, N., 169 n 18
Gintis, H.
   see Bowles and Gintis
Gintis, H. and Bowles, S., 181–2 n 10
Glass, D.V., 114
Gledhill, C., 184 n 11
Gleeson, D., 181 n 9
Glucksman, A., 158
Glucksmann, M., 173 n 7

Goldmann, L., 32, 33
Gramsci, A., 7, 10, 28, 40, 115, 118, 125,
   127, 129–44, 160–1, 168 n 5, 169 n 12,
   180 n 12, 181–3, 184 n 18 and n 19
Guirard, P., 174 n 17

Hall, S., 51, 83–4, 177 n 24
Hall, S., *et al.*, 169 n 12, 171 n 15, 173 n
   6, 174 n 21, 177 n 24, 182 n 30, 183 n
   38
Halsey, A.H., 3, 114
Hargreaves, D., 180 n 3
Hawkes, T., 173 n 1
Heath, S., 174 n 25
Hebdige, D., 58, 174 n 18 and n 24
Hegel, G.W., 8, 9, 76, 79
Henriques, J., *et al.*, 178 n 19
Hindess, B., 112, 155, 162
Hirst, P.Q., 16, 112, 155, 162, 169 n 19
Hoare, Q., 182 n 14
Hoare, Q. and Nowell Smith, G., 180 n
   12, 181 n 3–n 8
Hobsbawm, E., *et al.*, 180 n 5
Horney, K., 74

Isaacs, S., 99–100, 178 n 20

Jakobson, R., 48, 49, 74, 176 n 6
Jameson, F., 172 n 13
Jefferson, T.
   see Clarke and Jefferson
Jenks, C., 179 n 3
Jessop, B., 184 n 19
Johnson, R., 167 n 3, 169 n 18, 170 n 1,
   171 n 16
Joll, J., 143, 181 n 1, 183 n 37

Klein, 74
Kogan, M., 180 n 10
Kristeva, J., 79, 80, 84, 112

Lacan, J., 28, 45, 66, 68, 69–70, 71–85,
   87, 149, 152, 155–6, 158, 176 n 4, n 7,
   n 8 and n 13, 177 n 19–n 22, 185 n 23
Lacey, C., 180 n 3
Laclau, E., 161–5, 180 n 6, 184 n 19 and
   n 22, 184–5 n 23, 185 n 24
Laclau, E. and Mouffe, C., 185 n 25
Lane, H., 100, 178 n 22